The

EVERYTHING®
COLLEGE
SURVIVAL BOOK

P9-AGP-874

We Have EVERYTHING!

OVER **TWO MILLION** EVERYTHING BOOKS SOLD

Available wherever books are sold!

Everything® **After College Book**
$12.95, 1-55850-847-3

Everything® **Astrology Book**
$12.95, 1-58062-062-0

Everything® **Baby Names Book**
$12.95, 1-55850-655-1

Everything® **Baby Shower Book**
$12.95, 1-58062-305-0

Everything® **Barbeque Cookbook**
$12.95, 1-58062-316-6

Everything® **Bartender s Book**
$9.95, 1-55850-536-9

Everything® **Bedtime Story Book**
$12.95, 1-58062-147-3

Everything® **Bicycle Book**
$12.95, 1-55850-706-X

Everything® **Build Your Own Home Page**
$12.95, 1-58062-339-5

Everything® **Casino Gambling Book**
$12.95, 1-55850-762-0

Everything® **Cat Book**
$12.95, 1-55850-710-8

Everything® **Christmas Book**
$15.00, 1-55850-697-7

Everything® **College Survival Book**
$12.95, 1-55850-720-5

Everything® **Cover Letter Book**
$12.95, 1-58062-312-3

Everything® **Crossword and Puzzle Book**
$12.95, 1-55850-764-7

Everything® **Dating Book**
$12.95, 1-58062-185-6

Everything® **Dessert Book**
$12.95, 1-55850-717-5

Everything® **Dog Book**
$12.95, 1-58062-144-9

Everything® **Dreams Book**
$12.95, 1-55850-806-6

Everything® **Etiquette Book**
$12.95, 1-55850-807-4

Everything® **Family Tree Book**
$12.95, 1-55850-763-9

Everything® **Fly-Fishing Book**
$12.95, 1-58062-148-1

Everything® **Games Book**
$12.95, 1-55850-643-8

Everything® **Get-a-Job Book**
$12.95, 1-58062-223-2

Everything® **Get Published Book**
$12.95, 1-58062-315-8

Everything® **Get Ready For Baby Book**
$12.95, 1-55850-844-9

Everything® **Golf Book**
$12.95, 1-55850-814-7

Everything® **Guide to New York City**
$12.95, 1-58062-314-X

Everything® **Guide to Walt Disney World®, Universal Studios®, and Greater Orlando**
$12.95, 1-58062-404-9

Everything® **Guide to Washington D.C.**
$12.95, 1-58062-313-1

Everything® **Herbal Remedies Book**
$12.95, 1-58062-331-X

Everything® **Homeselling Book**
$12.95, 1-58062-304-2

Everything® **Homebuying Book**
$12.95, 1-58062-074-4

Everything® **Home Improvement Book**
$12.95, 1-55850-718-3

Everything® **Internet Book**
$12.95, 1-58062-073-6

Everything® **Investing Book**
$12.95, 1-58062-149-X

Everything® **Jewish Wedding Book**
$12.95, 1-55850-801-5

Everything® **Kids Money Book**
$9.95, 1-58062-322-0

Everything® **Kids Nature Book**
$9.95, 1-58062-321-2

Everything® **Kids Puzzle Book**
$9.95, 1-58062-323-9

Everything® **Low-Fat High-Flavor Cookbook**
$12.95, 1-55850-802-3

Everything® **Microsoft® Word 2000 Book**
$12.95, 1-58062-306-9

Everything® **Money Book**
$12.95, 1-58062-145-7

Everything® **One-Pot Cookbook**
$12.95, 1-58062-186-4

Everything® **Online Business Book**
$12.95, 1-58062-320-4

Everything® **Online Investing Book**
$12.95, 1-58062-338-7

Everything® **Pasta Book**
$12.95, 1-55850-719-1

Everything® **Pregnancy Book**
$12.95, 1-58062-146-5

Everything® **Pregnancy Organizer**
$15.00, 1-55850-336-0

Everything® **Resume Book**
$12.95, 1-58062-311-5

Everything® **Sailing Book**
$12.95, 1-58062-187-2

Everything® **Selling Book**
$12.95, 1-58062-319-0

Everything® **Study Book**
$12.95, 1-55850-615-2

Everything® **Tarot Book**
$12.95, 1-58062-191-0

Everything® **Toasts Book**
$12.95, 1-58062-189-9

Everything® **Total Fitness Book**
$12.95, 1-58062-318-2

Everything® **Trivia Book**
$12.95, 1-58062-143-0

Everything® **Tropical Fish Book**
$12.95, 1-58062-343-3

Everything® **Wedding Book, 2nd Edition**
$12.95, 1-58062-190-2

Everything® **Wedding Checklist**
$7.95, 1-58062-56-1

Everything® **Wedding Etiquette Book, 2nd Edition**
$7.95, 1-58062-454-5

Everything® **Wedding Organizer**
$15.00, 1-55850-828-7

Everything® **Wedding Shower Book, 2nd Edition**
$7.95, 1-58062-188-0

Everything® **Wedding Vows Book, 2nd Edition**
$7.95, 1-58062-455-3

Everything® **Wine Book**
$12.95, 1-55850-808-2

Everything® is a registered trademark of Adams Media Corporation

EVERYTHING KIDS'
Now Available!
Only $9.95 each

**For more information, or to order, call 800-872-5627
or visit everything.com**

Adams Media Corporation, 260 Center Street, Holbrook, MA 02343

The
EVERYTHING®
COLLEGE
SURVIVAL BOOK

From social life to study skills—everything
you need to know to fit right in—before you're a senior!

Jason Rich

ADAMS MEDIA CORPORATION
Holbrook, Massachusetts

Copyright ©1997, Adams Media Corporation.
All rights reserved. This book, or parts thereof,
may not be reproduced in any form without
permission from the publisher; exceptions are
made for brief excerpts used in published
reviews.

An Everything® Series Book.
Everything® is a registered trademark
of Adams Media Corporation.

Published by Adams Media Corporation
260 Center Street, Holbrook, MA 02343

ISBN: 1-55850-720-5

Printed in the United States of America.

J I H G

Library of Congress Cataloging-in-Publication Data
  Rich, Jason.
    The everything college survival book / Jason Rich.
      p.   cm.
    Includes index.
    ISBN 1-55850-720-5
    1. College student orientation—United States—
Handbooks, manuals, etc. I. Title. II. Series.
    LB2343.32.R53   1997
    378'.198—dc21   97-7844
                                                          CIP

This publication is designed to provide accurate
and authoritative information with regard to the
subject matter covered. It is sold with the
understanding that the publisher is not engaged
in rendering legal, accounting, or other professional advice. If legal advice or other expert
assistance is required, the services of a competent professional person should be sought.
— From a *Declaration of Principles* jointly
adopted by a Committee of the American Bar
Association and a Committee of Publishers
and Associations

Illustrations by Barry Littmann

*This book is available at quantity discounts
for bulk purchases. For information, call
1-800-872-5627 (in Massachusetts,
call 617-767-8100).*

Acknowledgments
Thanks to Pamela Liflander at Adams for
bringing me the idea for this book and
overseeing the entire project. My grati-
tude also goes out to Jeff Herman, my
literary agent, for making the introductions and getting this project started.

Thanks also to my parents for
putting me through college, and to Mark
Giordani and Ellen Bromfield, my two
closest friends, whom I met as a college
freshman back in 1985.

See the entire Everything® series at everything.com.

Contents

Introduction

Congratulations! You graduated from high school, made it through your SATs, and have been admitted to college. Although you probably don't realize it, you should consider yourself very privileged, because the percentage of Americans who actually go to college after high school is not as high as you might think. Just showing up for college orientation puts you a giant step forward in terms of your potential for success in your future career. Go ahead, pat yourself on the back. Pack your bags, and get ready for a fun-filled, challenging, and very rewarding two or four years.

What lies ahead are many classes that will require you to read thousands of pages worth of information, spend hundreds of hours studying facts and figures, and perform research on countless topics (either in the library or by going on-line). During the next several years, you're going to be challenged and exposed to many new experiences. You're also going to become more mature, meet new friends (some of whom could remain your close friends for the rest of your life), experience romance, and learn about your own strengths and weaknesses as a person. Somewhere along the way, you're also

going to prepare yourself for a lifelong career. This is what the college experience is about. But it's also about having fun and partying! No matter which college you attend, during the week you'll be expected to work hard; but when the weekends roll around, you'll hear people crank up their boom boxes and get into a party mood.

For some people, college represents major lifestyle changes. Some adapt easily and quickly to the new demands put upon them; others have to work extra hard and struggle a bit just to keep up. If you're part of this second group, there's no need to worry as long as you stay on top of your academic responsibilities and seek any extra help you need. The fact that you were admitted to college says a lot about your intelligence and what the admissions office thought about your potential. Now, however, it's up to you. To insure that you'll be able to keep up with and fulfill the academic demands of your classes, it is critical that you develop organizational skills. In addition, in order to achieve success and happiness in school, it is important to develop confidence in yourself.

College involves learning megaloads of information. Some of your studies will seem relevant to you at the time, and some will seem like a waste of time and totally worthless. The most important skill you will take away is the ability to teach yourself information and to discover how and where to find the answers that you need.

No matter what type of career you ultimately choose, you will not learn everything you need to know about it in college. In fact, once you land your first job in the real world, you'll quickly discover how much you don't know, even if you were a straight-A student. What your college education will provide are the tools and background knowledge you need to master whatever career you pursue.

One of the skills you should master while in school is the ability to communicate and work with other people, either on a one-on-one basis, or in a group. This is a skill that you'll need not only while in college but also when you land a job after graduation. The ability to

communicate, write clearly and concisely, and speak persuasively in front of people is an absolute must!

Throughout this book, many references are made to the use of the Internet—the Information Superhighway. Whenever possible, Web site addresses are provided so that you can obtain additional information on topics covered within these pages. The Internet is growing quickly and becoming an important resource. Thus, it's critical that you learn how to "surf the Net." *The Everything® College Survival Book* offers an introduction to computers and the Internet, but as a college student, you owe it to yourself to take an Introduction to the Internet class at your school, or at a local computer store, so that you can take full advantage in your personal and academic life of this high-tech resource. Just as in the latter part of the twentieth century calculators changed the way people do mathematics, computers and the Internet are destined to be the revolutionizing tools of the future. Take an active role to insure that you have the knowledge necessary to take full advantage of these high-tech tools.

Each person's college experience is totally different in terms of courses taken and day-to-day living experiences. If you attend a large school that's located in the heart of a major city, and your best friend from high school attends a small school in the suburbs of a midwestern state, you'll probably find very little similarity in your college experiences, except that you'll both be well-educated. People who attend small schools have experiences that are vastly different from those who attend large city universities that have no formal campus and thousands of students. Some schools offer a more general and well-rounded education; others offer specialties and more focused curriculums. The social scene and extracurricular activities at every college and university are also different, and what you experience as a student depends on your level of involvement.

The Everything® College Survival Book was written for you, an incoming freshman, as a general overview of what you can expect. Each chapter deals with a different topic or issue that you'll be facing as a college freshman—from packing for school to getting to know your roommate and selecting classes. This book will help you prepare to be a good student who is well-organized; however, it also covers issues that deal with the social aspects of school, like joining a fraternity or sorority, participating in sports, dating, and meeting new friends. After all, attending classes and studying are just a part of what your overall col-

lege experience will be about. Yes, earning good grades is important—it'll make your parents proud and help you to land a great job. However, it's important that you enjoy your college experience and have fun in the process of learning. *The Everything® College Survival Book* has several chapters that deal specifically with the many ways you can have fun while in school.

Instead of using this book as a source for answers to every question or situation that might arise once your college education begins, use this book as a tool for providing you with a good preview of what you can expect. It contains a lot of answers, but just as no college or university can totally prepare you for a career in the real world, no book can totally prepare you for everything you'll experience in college—not even a member of Dione Warwick's Psychic Friends Network could do that. As you start your life as a college student, begin it with a sense of excitement, confidence, and a strong will to succeed. Set your mind to earning good grades, but also to having a great time. Forget what people thought of you or what reputation you had in high school. College is one of the very few opportunities you'll have in life to get a fresh start.

The very best thing about having a college education is that it is one of the very few things in life that can never be lost or taken away from you (unless you sustain a serious head injury and get amnesia). During your lifetime, you might lose jobs. You might lose family members and friends. You might run into financial problems and lose your home, car, or personal belongings. But nobody can take away the knowledge you have in your head and your willingness to work hard and ultimately achieve great things.

Regardless of your background or financial situation, you have an incredible opportunity to make an exciting life for yourself. You can achieve your ultimate goals and dreams simply by obtaining a good, well-rounded college education and working hard. What lies ahead—your happiness, success, and financial well-being—is in your hands. But you're going to have to be persistent and work hard. Remember that what you get out of your college experience is up to you!

Good Luck!

DONT FORGET
☐ Computer
☑ Phone Directory
☐ Refridgerator
☐ Pajamas
☑ Teddy
☑ Camera
☐ Money (see Dad)
☑ Dave's Photo ♡
☐ Parents Photo
☐ Aspirin

CHAPTER

PACKING FOR COLLEGE

GETTING YOUR STUFF TOGETHER AND GETTING IT TO THE DORM

f you were about to go on a camping trip or on a mountain climbing expedition, your comfort and survival would depend on your packing the right supplies and equipment. You don't want to take along too much, but at the same time, there are certain things you're definitely going to need and want. The same rules apply when you pack for school. Begin packing for college early. This will help to insure that you bring along everything you'll need. If you rush to pack and throw everything you own into a bunch of boxes or suitcases a day before you have to leave, you're going to forget stuff. Most importantly, keep a list of everything you pack. This will keep you from thinking that your stuff got lost, help keep you organized, and make packing and unpacking easier.

Break up your packing into two categories: your clothing, and your other stuff. Begin by packing your clothing.

What are you going to need? To answer this question, first consider the climate. Are you attending a school in Florida or California, for example, where it's always warm, or is your school located in New England or some locale where winter can get pretty harsh? Also, determine how often you will be able to go home. If you'll be visiting home every few weeks, you don't need to pack your entire wardrobe now. Only bring what you'll need for the weather right away. Keep in mind, in late August or September, when the fall semester begins, summer is just about over, so unless your school is in a warm climate, pack for fall.

Here's a list of the articles of clothing and accessories you should consider packing. Again, think about the climate you'll be living in, as well as your personal tastes:

- Backpack/book bag
- Bathing suit
- Bathrobe
- Belt(s)
- Blouses
- Casual shoes
- Dress shoes
- Dresses
- Fashion accessories
- Gloves, scarf(s), hats
- Jacket (wind breaker)
- Jeans
- Jewelry (Don't bring anything that's very valuable or that can't be replaced.)
- Pajamas
- Pantyhose
- Pocketbook(s)/handbag(s)

○ Raincoat
○ Shirts (long-sleeve)
○ Shorts
○ Skirts
○ Slacks (khaki pants)
○ Sneakers
○ Socks
○ Sport jacket and tie
○ Sweaters
○ Sweatshirt(s) and sweatsuit
○ T-shirts
○ Turtleneck shirts or sweaters
○ Umbrella
○ Underwear (boxers, briefs, athletic supporters, bras, panties, thermal underwear, etc.)
○ Watch
○ Winter coat

Here is a list of the toiletries you'll need to bring:

○ Bucket (to carry toiletries to and from the communal bathroom—you probably won't have your own!)
○ Contact lenses and related supplies
○ Cosmetics

○ Deodorant
○ First-aid kit (aspirin, adhesive bandages, etc.)
○ Hair care products
○ Hair dryer
○ Hairbrush and comb
○ Laundry detergent and fabric softener
○ Medication(s) (and refillable prescriptions)
○ Nail file/clippers
○ Perfume, cologne
○ Shampoo and conditioner
○ Shaving gear
○ Soap
○ Tissues and handkerchiefs
○ Toothbrush, dental floss, mouthwash, toothpaste
○ Towels (bring extras)
○ Washcloths

Once your clothing is packed, it's time to pack the rest of your stuff. Before doing this, give your soon-to-be-roommate(s) a call and see what they're bringing. You'll only need one TV, one stereo, and one microwave, for example. Here's a list of some stuff you should definitely bring along (or at least consider packing):

- Alarm clock (Make sure it's reliable and has a battery backup.)
- Answering machine
- Basic tools (hammer and screwdrivers)
- Batteries (variety of sizes)
- Bedspread
- Blanket(s)
- Bottle opener
- Bulletin board
- Calculator (Get a recommendation from your school about what type of calculator you'll need.)
- Calendar/student planner
- Camera and film
- Clothes hangers
- Coffeemaker and mugs
- Computer
- Computer paper, supplies, and cables
- Computer printer
- Computer software and manuals
- Desk lamp and light bulbs
- Dictionary and thesaurus
- Envelopes and stamps
- Extension cord and adapter(s)
- Fan (if your dorm doesn't have air conditioning)
- Flashlight
- Folders
- Forks, knives, etc.
- Glue and thumb tacks

- Highlighting markers (several colors)
- Iron and portable ironing board
- Laundry bag (Put your name on the bag!)
- Mattress pad (You don't want to think about who has been sleeping in your bed or what they did on that mattress!)
- Microwave oven, popcorn maker
- Pads of paper
- Paper clips
- Pens and pencils
- Photo of your family, pet(s), boyfriend/girlfriend
- Pillow(s)
- Posters for dorm walls (as well as other room decorations)
- Reading light (for the bed)
- Ruler
- Scissors
- Sewing kit
- Sheets (bring extras)
- Sporting goods (tennis racquet, baseball glove, skis, etc.)
- Stapler and staples
- Stationery

- Stereo, portable radio, or cassette player and tapes, CDs, etc. (Headphones are a must!)
- Storage boxes, shelves, closet organizer

- Tape (clear and packing tape)
- Telephone message pads (if you'll have roommates)
- Three-ring binder(s) (one per subject)

As you start packing, think about how little room you have in your dorm. Dorms don't offer students a lot of space, especially if you're going to have roommates. A typical dorm will provide you with a standard size closet, a three- or four-drawer dresser, a desk, a chair, and a bed—so much for elegant living. It'll be up to your creativity and organizational skills to make your dorm comfortable.

As you place articles of clothing in your suitcase, in your duffel bag, or in a box, think about where you're going to store it—in the closet, in the dresser, or under your bed. Here are some things to think about when packing:

- If you know you won't wear something regularly, don't pack it.
- Don't pack too many articles of clothing that require ironing, special care, or dry cleaning.
- Bring plenty of the basics, like underwear, socks, jeans, T-shirts, sweatshirts, and pajamas. These are the things you'll need plenty of. Mom won't be doing your laundry every few days, so pack extras! A ten-day supply (or more) of underwear and socks will come in handy.
- Pack clothing that you're both comfortable with and comfortable wearing. When you visit your school, study the types of clothes the other students wear. Unlike in high school, at most colleges the latest designer fashions and being totally stylish are not priorities. Most college students are on a budget and can't afford expensive designer clothing. You'll probably find that casual and more basic attire (jeans and a T-shirt) is the norm.
- Bring along one or two formal outfits for "special occasions."
- Don't forget shoes and sneakers. Bring along more than one pair of shoes, but don't go overboard. You'll probably be doing a lot of walking, especially if attending a school with a large campus and you don't have a car. Make sure your shoes are comfortable. At UCLA, for example, most of the classrooms are located about a fifteen-minute walk from the dorms.
- Be yourself. Dress in a way that shows who you really are, or how you would like to be perceived.

○ Toilet paper (Have your own stash for emergencies. Don't rely on your school to keep the bathrooms stocked!)
○ TV (optional)
○ VCR (optional)
○ Video game system (optional)

Since you haven't yet been to college, it's hard to predict what additional items you may need. Bring along some extra cash, or make an allowance in your budget, for extra necessities that you can purchase once you get to school. If you can, talk to a few upperclassmen at your school, and ask them for suggestions on what else you might want or need.

Once you've gotten everything packed, you've got to get it all to school. You can pack up your car and drive, ship stuff via UPS (or another courier), or bring it on an airplane, bus, or train. If you're taking a plane, bus, or train, keep in mind that there are luggage restrictions. For example, most airlines allow you to check two suitcases and have two small carry-ons. They charge up to $50 per bag beyond those limits. If you choose to ship your things via UPS, be sure that you pack carefully, address your boxes correctly, and insure the packages.

Unless you're going to school in the middle of nowhere, chances are there will be a mall nearby where you can buy anything you forget. At the very least, every school has a bookstore that sells the basics. As a last resort, you can always call your parents and have them send whatever you left behind.

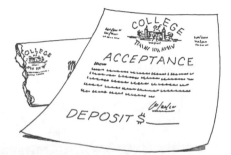

CHAPTER

2

PAYING FOR YOUR EDUCATION

YOU GOT ADMITTED, NOW COUGH UP THE CASH

veryone stresses the importance of a college education, yet few people are willing to discuss how someone is supposed to pay for it. The tuition for colleges and universities across America is skyrocketing, while the availability of scholarships and student loans is dwindling. Every year over fifteen million American families are faced with college tuition, and the availability of funds is often a serious consideration that sometimes impacts where a student can attend school. Your college education can cost anywhere from $5,000 to $35,000 per year.

National Student Resources, an independent guidance counseling service, helps families develop plans for paying for their children's college education by drawing from a continually updated database containing three hundred thousand sources of educational funding. The company provides students with a tailored report based on the student's specific financial, academic, and personal history.

Richard Laiden, the President of National Student Resources, understands many options available to college students and their families when it comes time to develop a financial plan for paying for a college education. He and his staff help students and their families determine how to profile themselves when dealing with a school's financial aid office. In addition, they pinpoint scholarships for which an individual student is qualified.

Richard stresses that if you're going to pay for a college education, you're going to have to plan well, pull out all of the stops, and spend a considerable amount of time doing research to find the scholarship money that's available to you. The alternative is to take out huge student loans and graduate with a large debt. "The biggest problem most students and their families face is a total lack of knowledge about ho the whole financial aid and scholarship system works. It is a process and a system, and you can't rely on the financial aid office at a college to help you. Families need to profile their assets in a certain way to be eligible for scholarship money, and that requires early planning."

Financial planners generally agree that early preparation and long-term savings by parents and students is the best plan for paying for college. If, however, the money you have available isn't enough, don't panic! There are plenty of scholarship and loan opportunities available to current or soon-to-be college students that aren't based on academic achievement or your family's financial situation.

If you're in need of financial assistance, and you're about to begin your college education, be prepared to spend some time actively seeking out scholarship and loan opportunities. Begin by setting up an appointment with the financial aid administrators at the college you'll be attending or those you'll be applying to. If you're still in your senior year of high school, check with the guidance counselor at your school. Be sure to visit a library or bookstore and check out the many directories of government and private institutions that offer college scholarships and loans. On the Internet, use any Web search engine (such as Yahoo! at http://www.yahoo.com) and enter the keywords *Scholarships* and *Financial Aid* to locate many sources of funds.

The single largest source of financial aid is the federal government, but state governments, colleges, and private organizations also offer many forms of financial aid to college students. There are basically three types of financial aid that you can apply for:

1. *Gift-aid, grants and scholarships.* These are monies that do not have to be repaid. The federal government funds two of the largest higher education grant programs—the Pell Grant Program and the Supplemental Education Opportunity Grant (SEOG) Program. These two programs are designed to assist the most financially needy students. Every community offers many sources for scholarships and grants that are not based on financial need or academic performance. To find out about them, contact your local house of worship, local foundations, civic groups, professional organizations (such as unions), local Veteran's Administration, and other community organizations.

2. *Work-study programs.* Students can earn money while they are in college by working part time on campus or in the community. These programs are sponsored by the colleges and by the local, state, and federal government.

Consult the financial aid office at your college for information. High school graduates can earn education awards through a federal program called AmeriCorps National and Community Service; by working before, during, or after college, students can fund their education or repay their student loans. Call (800) 942-2677 for details about this program.

3. *Education loans.* These loans must be repaid, usually with interest. There are many sources for obtaining education loans, including the government, banks, and other lending institutions. Federal Stafford loans come from the federal government and are low-interest loans that are made to undergraduate and graduate students who attend accredited colleges and universities at least half time. These loans are based on financial need and are determined by a federal formula. Students who don't qualify for subsidized Stafford loans can get unsubsidized Stafford loans, regardless of their family's income. With an unsubsidized Stafford loan, students are responsible for the interest during in-school and deferment periods.

It is possible to defer making payments until after graduation; however, the accrued interest is added to the loan principal, which ultimately increases the total repayment amount.

Other types of government loans available to students are Federal PLUS loans and Federal Perkins loans. Consult with the financial aid office at your school for details about how to qualify for these loans. For more information about federal and state government loan programs, call (800) 4-FED-AID.

Yet another major source for student loans is Sally Mae, which is a financial services corporation that specializes in funding education, and currently funds about 40 percent of all insured student loans outstanding. Sally Mae has education servicing centers located around the country and is headquartered in Washington, D.C. Sally Mae offers a toll-free College Answer telephone service that provides current information about college cost, financial aid programs available, financial assistance eligibility, and the application process. This service also offers free assistance in completing and submitting the Free Application for Federal Student Aid (FAFSA). For more information about Sally Mae and the College Answer service, call (800) 222-7182, or visit the Sally Mae Web site at http://www.saliemae.com.

The United State military (Army, Navy, Air Force, and Marines) also offers programs designed to help college students pay for their education. Each division of the military offers a variety of different opportunities that allows you to earn money for college while being patriotic and supporting your country. For opportunities available from the U.S. Army, call (800) USA-ARMY. On the Internet, check out the Army's Web site at http://www.goarmy.com. To reach the U.S. Navy, call (800) USA-NAVY. And to reach the U.S. Marines, call (800) 342-2408. You can also visit the recruiting center in your town or city. To find the location of a nearby recruiting center, check your local phone book.

Most high school guidance offices and libraries offer lots of free information about federal and state scholarship programs that are available. This is a wonderful place to start the learning process. Within any community, there are many clubs, religious institutions, and professional organizations that offer

scholarship money. "Parents and students should begin seriously planning and applying for scholarships during a student's junior year in high school," adds Richard. "The admissions office and the financial aid office at the majority of colleges and universities now work together closely. As a result, it is critical that students profile themselves correctly to the college or university that they are interested in attending. For example, the 'eagerness syndrome' can have a negative impact on a students chances for receiving scholarship money from a college or university. The more eager you are to attend a school, the less scholarship money that will be offered. In other words, demonstrating a strong eagerness to attend a school can actually be detrimental in some cases when it comes to receiving campus-based aide."

When choosing a college or university to attend, there are many things that a student should carefully evaluate. If paying for the education is going to be an issue, the student and his or her family should pay attention to each school's campus-based aide programs, based on what the student hopes to study.

Once you have a general understanding of how financial aid and scholarship programs work, it is critical that the student's assets are allocated correctly. "For example, if Grandma gives $10,000 to the person about to be entering college, and that money is placed in the student's name, that can severely impact the financial need-based process. You have to prove need, and need is by definition. Need doesn't mean that you're destitute. It's calculated based on a formula that involves the income of the parents and the assets of the student. The government has taken steps to protect parents so that they are not required to spend their retirement funds to pay for their child's education," explains Richard.

One of the biggest misconceptions about student aid is that you have to be super bright or super poor to receive scholarships. That's simply not the case if you understand the process. "Scholarships go to people who know how to get them, understand the system, and start the application process for these funds early on. If you want to receive scholarship money, you're going to have to put in the time and work at it. The result, however, will be that you'll save thousands of dollars. If you pull out all of the stops, you have the right information, and you're motivated, just about any student will be able to find a way to pay for college. Every student's first step should be visiting with a high school guidance counselor and/or a college's financial aid office. The biggest mistake parents and students make is thinking that they can't get scholarship money, so they don't bother to apply for it. Money is available in the private sector for A, B, and even C students, as well as for students whose parents make a respectable income," adds Richard.

There are many ways to find information about private sector scholarship programs. For $129 you can use the services of National Student Resources. They will develop a customized list of scholarship money that you can apply for. To contact National Student Resources, call (800) 915-CASH. A student will typically receive a report listing between twenty and seventy sources of grants and scholarships for which they could qualify.

If you have access to the Internet, use a search engine such as YAHOO! (http://www.yahoo.com), and run a search based on the keyword *Scholarships*. This will provide you

with a listing of Web sites for specific scholarship programs that you might not already be aware of. For example, did you know that Coca-Cola has a scholarship program? You can find out more by visiting the company's Web site (http://www.coca-cola.com/scholars) or by calling (800) 306-COKE. Each year, Coca-Cola awards 150 high school seniors with a scholarship based on merit. (This includes 50 $20,000 scholarships and 100 $4,000 scholarships.) Coca-Cola evaluates a student's "merit" based on leadership in school, civic, and other extracurricular activities, academic achievement, and motivation to serve and succeed. The company states that "personal character is always important."

For computer users, Bullseye Systems offers a program for personal computers (PCs) called "$scholarship $elect." It contains a database of over 80,000 scholarships that are available from colleges and universities, professional societies, ethnic associations, national associations, nonprofit organizations, states, union affiliations, company sponsors, and religious organizations. This software costs $56 (including shipping and handling) and can be ordered directly from Bullseye Systems, 2268 Westmoreland Drive, San Jose, CA 95124 or call (408) 266-9226.

Another CD-ROM-based software package for PCs, called Cash For Class, offers a one-step college scholarship program for locating potential financing, and contacting those sources with customized, printed application letters and mailing labels. The database within this software offers information on over 9,000 scholarships. Cash For Class is priced at $29.95. For more information, call (800) 205-9581.

Daniel J. Cassidy, the President of National Scholarship Research Service, offers a book called *The Scholarship Book*. It contains detailed information on over one hundred thousand scholarships. The book costs $32.95 and is available at bookstores or by calling (800) 947-7700.

CHAPTER

3

TIPS FOR EARNING

SOME EXTRA CASH

College is expensive, and even if you are lucky enough to have your tuition and dorm room paid for, you're still going to want some spending money. Here are some ideas on how to earn extra cash by working on a part-time basis during the school year:

1. Get a part-time job at a local retail store or fast food-restaurant. Malls, shopping centers, and fast-food restaurants are ideal sources of part-time employment. If you're looking to work flexible hours and aren't looking for anything glamorous in terms of employment opportunities, a job in retail or fast food is an excellent way to earn extra cash. In your junior and senior years of college, however, don't just take any job. Try to get a job in the industry you hope to enter when you graduate. This will provide you with valuable work experience that will look great on your resume. For example, if you hope to go on to law school and become an attorney, try to get a job working part-time in a law office.

2. Work as a waiter/waitress in a restaurant. This requires skill, and usually you must be available to work evenings and weekends. If you work in an up-scale restaurant, you can earn good tips plus a salary.

3. Is there an academic subject that you excel in? Become a tutor. If so, you could help your fellow students and earn some money by tutoring. Tutors charge by the hour. In this type of work, you are your own boss and work whatever hours you want. To find students to tutor, put signs on your campus bulletin boards. Also speak with a few of your professors and ask them to recommend you to students as a tutor.

4. Type papers for students. Typing someone's paper is very different from writing it. Since not everyone knows how to type and format with a word processor, making a research paper look good after it's been written can take someone with no typing or computer skills several hours. By providing a typing service, you can charge people by the page or by the hour and save them valuable time. One of the best ways to find clients is to post signs on campus bulletin boards.

5. Are you a computer whiz? Offer fellow students help learning to

use their computer. It's now a requirement at just about every college and university for students to own a computer, however, not all students know how to use their computers; You can teach students how to operate their computers, surf the Internet, and use software. Charge for your services by the hour.

6. Get a job on-campus. In conjunction with the financial aid office, most schools hire students to work in on-campus jobs. To find out more about these employment opportunities, contact your school's financial aid or student employment office.

7. Work as a campus representative for a Spring Break travel company or another organization. These jobs are offered by companies that market their products or services directly to college students. Your job often involves selling products/services to your fellow students. You'll often receive commissions for your sales, plus added incentives, like a free Spring Break trip for every predetermined number of trip packages that you sell. Employment opportunities like these are often posted on campus bulletin boards. Before accepting a position as a campus representative for any product or service, make sure the company you'll be working for is totally reputable— after all, you'll be selling stuff to your peers.

8. Become a "mystery shopper." Agencies across America hire people of all ages to go undercover and act as mystery shoppers in stores. As a mystery shopper, you will be told by your employer what types of things you should look for and evaluate while you're doing your undercover shopping work. You'll be expected to write a report on your findings. The best thing about this type of work is that you can work whatever hours you want. It's an excellent part-time opportunity for someone who enjoys shopping. Just one of the many "mystery shopper" agencies

that hires people from around the country is Imaginus Training & Development, at (716) 635–9146.

9. Are you good with tools or do you enjoy working outdoors? You can help people in your community by performing odd jobs or doing lawn work. To get this type of work, post signs on bulletin boards in supermarkets, hardware stores, and other public places. You can also place small advertisements in local newspapers. To avoid the legal hassles of having the right type of insurance, etc., get a job working for an agency that uses part-time or freelance outdoor workers.

10. Work as a babysitter or mother's helper for families in your community.

11. Check the "Help Wanted" ads in your local newspaper for part-time employment opportunities and check with the Career Planning Office at your school.

Money Saving Tips

Once you've started earning some extra money, you'll want to make it last. First, develop a personal budget for yourself. Make a resolution to stick to it. Using a note pad or spreadsheet software on your computer, keep track of all the money you spend in a typical week. Next, evaluate this list and look for ways you can save money.

If you start running low on cash, don't rely on your credit cards to bail you out of a tough financial situation. Unless it's an absolute emergency and you know you'll be able to pay off the credit card debt quickly, don't rely on credit cards. Having large outstanding balances on your credit cards costs serious money, due to the high interest fees charged on an ongoing basis.

Second, try to put money aside (even just a few dollars) each week or month for emergencies. There are many ways you can save money while in school. Here are just a few easy things you can do:

○ Make your long-distance telephone calls in the evenings and on weekends when the rates are cheaper, unless you're on a one-rate-plan. Instead of calling a boyfriend/girlfriend every day, call two or three times a week and send e-mail on the days you don't phone. Avoid using a telephone charge card. These cards often carry a surcharge of 75 cents (or more) per call, especially if used from a pay phone. When calling from a pay phone, always use a long distance phone company that you know, such as AT&T, MCI, or Sprint, to avoid additional surcharges. From any pay phone, dial 1-0-ATT-0 and then the telephone number, or dial 1-(800) CALL-ATT to ensure that you'll be using AT&T's long distance service. To save additional money, don't accept collect calls.

o Instead of going to a movie theater in the evening and paying full price to see a movie, see a discount matinee. Better yet, rent a movie on videocassette and watch it with friends.

o Instead of eating out at restaurants, make food in your dorm or stick with the meal plan at your school. If you've already paid for a meal plan, you might as well eat the slop most school dining rooms try to pass off as food. Don't worry, you won't die from the stuff. But remember, even eating at fast food restaurants or ordering take-out gets expensive.

o If you smoke cigarettes, stop. This alone will save you a fortune!

o If you're of legal drinking age, cut down on the purchase of alcoholic beverages. Instead of buying your own, go to fraternity parties where beverages are supplied.

o Attend on-campus activities and parties so you don't have to pay cover charges at nightclubs and discos.

o Wait for sales and use discount coupons offered by major department stores when buying clothing. Also, buy clothing and accessories that you can mix and match in order to create multiple outfits. Buy clothing in styles and colors that can be worn during multiple seasons and that will last. Buy clothing that's washable and does not require costly dry cleaning.

o Use coupons at the supermarket and buy store-brand (generic) products when possible. Often these products are identical to the popular brand-name products, so check the ingredient labels. Also, it's almost always cheaper to buy larger containers of food and household products.

o If you use an on-line service (such as America On-line) or an

Internet service provider with your computer, choose an unlimited, flat-rate use plan, so you don't rack up large on-line bills.

○ Use your bike or in-line skates whenever possible to avoid using a car or paying for a bus or taxi.

○ For entertainment, take advantage of free cultural events and activities in your college community.

○ When you visit your hairstylist, choose a hairstyle that is simple and low-maintenance. You don't want to be forced to visit the salon often or have to pay big bucks for a lot of extra haircare products.

○ Instead of buying new textbooks, buy used books whenever possible. Don't share books, however, with a friend or roommate. You always want to have your own set of textbooks. At the end of the semester, sell your books back to the bookstore to earn a bit of extra cash.

○ When you go to the store or Mall, avoid making spontaneous purchases. Only buy items that you need. Periodically, if you have some extra cash, you can reward yourself by buying something frivolous. It's very easy to go into a store (or watch home shopping shows on TV) and buy stuff you don't really need, and discover later that you don't really want.

○ If you're a heavy coffee drinker, buy a coffee machine for you dorm room and avoid buying individual cups of pre-made coffee from vending machines or coffee shops.

CHAPTER

4

DEVELOPING CREDIT

PASS THE PLASTIC!

More than 8 million of America's college students have some type of credit card. Do you?

People are using more and more credit, which means that the banks and financial institutions that issue credit cards are raking in megabucks. To constantly increase the number of credit cards being issued, many banks and financial institutions have begun targeting college students, offering special incentives for students with no previous credit history.

Before you start filling out applications for Visa, MasterCard, American Express, Discover, and Diners Club, it is vital that you have a good understanding of what having credit is all about. If you somehow screw up your credit rating (which is rather easy to do), your chances of getting credit in the future can be shot for up to seven years.

According to American Express, "Credit is a contract based on your promise to pay in the future for goods and services you receive today. It's a contract based on your credit record, ability to pay, the security or collateral you have, and the condition of the merchandise. Credit is a responsibility and a resource—but it's not a right."

American Express has developed a special program called Credit Ready?

Five Essential Lessons Before Starting To Use Credit. Part of this program involves a ten-question quiz that can

WHAT'S THE DIFFERENCE BETWEEN A CHARGE CARD AND A CREDIT CARD?

According to American Express, a charge card requires full payment of the bill each month, without interest. The American Express card and Diners Club card are examples. A credit card is a card that allows you to pay a portion or all of the outstanding amount each month, with interest. A credit card almost always has a pre-defined credit limit, which is the amount of credit you are authorized to use. A secured credit card is available when a consumer uses savings or other collateral to guarantee the credit card. The limit of credit is based on the amount of collateral available. Many banks now offer Visa or MasterCards that are linked directly to your checking account. These are, in effect, debit cards, because when you make a purchase using this type of card, the charge is immediately and automatically deducted from your checking account.

help you determine if you're financially responsible enough to have your own credit cards. As you read these questions, you may be able to pick out the obvious best answer; but instead of doing that, choose the answer that most honestly fits your personality and spending habits. Honestly answering each question will help you to determine how financially responsible you are. For each question, circle your answer.

1. If your aunt gave you $50 for your birthday, what would you do?
   A. Deposit it into your savings bank
   B. Buy yourself something you need
   C. Consider it extra spending money
   D. Treat yourself to a night out

2. If you got a new job that paid $75 a week, what would you do?
   A. Open a savings account immediately
   B. Wait until your first paycheck and then decide what to do
   C. Make a plan to pay off your bills
   D. Start shopping for a new CD player

3. When you owe somebody money, how do you feel?
   A. Uncomfortable until it's all paid off
   B. Aware of the debt but not uncomfortable about it
   C. Interested in paying it off as soon as it's convenient
   D. Willing to pay but not in a hurry

4. If your best friend asked to borrow $40 from you, what would you do?
   A. Lend it but only in case of an emergency
   B. Be happy to lend it
   C. Be willing to lend it but want to know when you'd get it back
   D. Not be willing to lend it

5. When you buy something, what do you do?
   A. Make sure of all the details before you buy
   B. Ask some questions but not too many
   C. Listen to what the salesperson tells you
   D. Assume everything will be okay

6. If a bill were due on the first of the month, when would you mail the payment?
   A. At least ten days in advance to be sure that it gets there on time
   B. About five days before it's due
   C. A day or so before it's due
   D. When you had the money

7. How often do you buy something on impulse?
   A. Never
   B. Very rarely
   C. Sometimes
   D. Almost always

8. If you had a credit card and owed $100 and had the cash to pay, what would you do?
   A. Pay the bill in full
   B. Pay $50 and keep the rest for spending money
   C. Pay $25 and put the rest in savings
   D. Pay the minimum of $10 and use the rest for other bills

9. If you had a credit card and were shopping for something, what would you do?
   A. Consider price, cost of credit, and the quality of the item
   B. Just shop for the best price
   C. Buy the best quality, regardless of price
   D. Buy what you want even if it's expensive

10. When you have $20 in your pocket, what would you do?
   A. Hang on to it, no matter what
   B. Spend it, but only if you must
   C. Spend it on something you really want
   D. Spend it on just about anything

Okay, it's time to rate yourself and see how you made out.

Each *A* answer is worth five points.
Each *B* answer is worth three points.
Each *C* answer is worth two points.
Each *D* answer is worth one point.

Now tally up your score. Obviously, if it turns out that you're not as financially minded as you might have thought, you can learn to change your spending habits rather easily, so don't think you're doomed to failure and a life of credit problems. On the contrary; if you learn how to manage your finances now, you could make out extremely well in the long run.

Here's how you evaluate your score:

o If your score is between 45 and 50, the folks at American Express who developed this quiz think you're a financial wizard. You're both money smart and credit conscious.

o If you scored between 30 and 44, you're a smart shopper. You're clever about money, but could be more sensitive to credit costs. It could save you plenty of money in the long run.

o If you scored between 19 and 29, you're a casual consumer. You're too relaxed about price and credit terms. There could be trouble ahead unless you become more money minded.

o Finally, if you scored between 1 and 18, you're a big spender. You like to buy stuff, but you're not concerned about getting the best value. Be careful, because you could easily run into credit problems.

Some of the things you can do to help control your spending include:

o Avoid buying things impulsively.
o Don't charge more than you budgeted or more than you can afford.

o Don't pay penalties or other fees without being aware of them.
o Avoid just making minimum credit card payments and carrying high outstanding credit balances (which means you're paying lots of interest).
o Don't buy items that wear out before you've paid for them. You could end up purchasing a replacement while you're still paying for the first purchase.
o Never spend up to your line of credit, because if you need some additional credit for an emergency, you'll wind up paying a higher price for it.
o Don't apply for and accept credit cards based on offers that sound too good to be true. Always read, and make sure you understand, the fine print on all credit applications. For example, if a local electronics store offers you a store credit card with no interest and no fees for six months, you'll often be billed for all interest and fees if your balance is not paid in full by the very first day of the seventh month. Before making a large purchase, think about how quickly you plan to pay for that purchase and how much

interest you will ultimately be paying as a result if you maintain a balance on your credit card as you pay off that purchase. You can buy, for example, a $1000 stereo system with a credit card and have a very low monthly payment of $20 or $30; but by the time that purchase is paid off, you could easily wind up paying 150 percent (or more) of the original purchase price for the product.

Before you start applying for credit cards, carefully read that tiny print that's on all applications. You'll notice that credit card and charge card applications (whether they're for a Visa, MasterCard, Discover, American Express, Diners Club, gas station credit card, or department store credit card) often ask the same few questions:

- Your name
- Your current and previous addresses
- Years/months at current address
- Phone number
- Social Security number
- Date of birth
- Mother's maiden name
- Annual personal gross income
- Additional personal income
- Employer/college attending
- Bank account information (savings and checking)

When you're filling out credit card/charge card applications, always fill in answers to all of the questions asked. Don't leave anything blank, and NEVER lie on an application. If you have questions about how to fill out a specific application, call the telephone number that's listed on the application.

American Express has developed this partial glossary of terms to help you understand those all-important buzzwords that appear in the credit card applications:

Amount Due. Generally, the minimum monthly payment you must make, not the total amount you owe.

Annual Fee. The annual membership fee, if any, of having a credit or charge card.

Annual Percentage Rate (APR). The cost of credit for one year expressed as a percentage.

Available Credit. The unused portion of the credit that falls within the consumer's applicable credit limit, if any.

Billing Cycle. The number of days between your last bill and your current bill—usually twenty-eight to thirty-one days.

Billing Statement. Your periodic credit card bill, which describes and summarizes all the outstanding balances, purchases, payments, credits, finance charges, and other transactions for the month.

Cash Advance. A loan taken out by charging an amount of cash to your credit card. Interest for cash advances is usually higher than it is for purchases, and generally there is no grace period, so interest begins accumulating immediately. There can also be a transaction fee for cash advances.

Co-Sign. To sign a credit agreement with someone and agree to share the debt with that person or assume the debt if the other person defaults and doesn't pay. As a college student, NEVER co-sign a credit card application with a friend, romantic interest, or even a relative who isn't financially responsible, or you could be the one who winds up paying the other person's bills; failure to pay will destroy your credit rating.

You can receive one or two copies of your credit report, free of charge, each year. In addition, you can obtain a copy of your credit report if you are denied credit after completing an application for a credit/charge card. To obtain a copy of your personal credit report, or for information about your credit report, call one of the three credit reporting agencies:

Equifax	(800) 685-1111
TRW	(800) 392-1122
Trans Union	(800) 851-2674

Credit Report. Credit reports are the foundation of the consumer credit system. Large and small businesses around the country send regular customer credit usage to the three primary credit reporting companies: TRW, Equifax, and Trans Union. These credit reporting companies use credit reports to create detailed, up-to-date credit records on every person who uses credit. These individual credit records are used to provide credit reports to businesses that are considering granting credit to someone.

Due Date. The day a payment is due to a creditor. After that date, a late fee can be charged and the payment can be recorded as late or the account can be considered delinquent. WARNING: Paying credit or charge card bills late will damage your credit rating and in the long term can hurt your chances of receiving additional credit or charge cards, a car loan, or even a mortgage.

Finance Charge. The percentage charge that is applied to the daily or monthly balances as described in the credit agreement.

Fixed Interest Rate. An interest rate that does not change.

Grace Period. The period of time, generally between twenty and twenty-five days, from the billing date of your last charge or credit card bill to the due date of your current bill, when you pay in full without being charged interest. Some cards do not offer a grace period. Others only have a grace period if there was an outstanding balance on the account at the start of the billing cycle. Generally there is no grace period for cash advances.

Late Payment Fee. A charge added to an account if a required payment is not received by a specific date.

Minimum Monthly Payment. The smallest payment you can make to maintain your account on current status. If you somehow totally mess up your personal finances and wind up charging your credit card(s) to their limit, at the very

least, ALWAYS pay the minimum monthly payment that's listed on your statement. Failing to do this will quickly destroy your overall credit rating. If you absolutely have no money and can't make the minimum monthly payment, pay whatever you can, but first, call up the credit card company and explain your situation. Work with the credit card company to develop a repayment plan that you can deal with. Whatever you do, NEVER ignore credit card statements and hope they'll disappear—they won't, and you'll quickly find yourself having financial problems as well as legal ones that are extremely difficult to remedy. Remember, anytime you fail to make a payment on a credit/charge card bill, this negative information is reported to the credit report agencies. Once this happens, negative information is placed in your credit report. Your credit report is something that is updated each month, and stays with you for your entire life. Thus, it's extremely important that you maintain a positive credit history.

Monthly Periodic Rate. The rate of interest per month, calculated by dividing the Annual Percentage Rate (APR) by 12.

Over-Limit Fee. A charge imposed on some credit accounts for spending over the credit limit.

Pay Due. The status of a bill when the minimum payment has not been received by the due date.

Periodic Rate. The interest rate derived in relation to a specific amount of time.

Previous Balance. The amount you still owe after last month's payments and charges were added to your balance.

Principal. The amount of money you owe, not including the interest due on it.

Revolving Credit. A credit agreement that allows consumers to pay all or part of the outstanding balance on a loan or credit card. As credit is paid off, it becomes available again to use for another purchase or cash advance.

Transaction Fee. An extra charge for various credit activities, such as using an automatic teller machine (ATM) or receiving a cash advance.

Variable Interest Rate. An interest rate that changes up or down on a set schedule based on an economic index, such as the prime rate.

Zero Balance. When the outstanding balance is paid and there are no new charges during a billing cycle.

Here are some tips for maintaining good credit:

- Once you apply for and receive credit/charge cards, always keep them in a safe place.
- Never give your credit card number or PIN (personal identification number) to anyone.

- Keep all of your ATM and sales receipts.
- When making a purchase with a credit/charge card, before signing the charge slip, make sure all of the amounts (especially the total) are correct.
- After signing the charge slip, take your copy and destroy the carbon that's in between the copies. The carbon contains your credit card number and your signature—an easy blueprint for someone to rip you off.
- Never give your credit card information over the phone to strangers. Of course, if you're ordering something by phone that you saw in a catalog, for example, that's okay.
- Always keep track of all your credit expenses. Pay all of your bills on time.
- If you spot errors in your credit/charge card statement, or if a credit/charge card gets lost or stolen, call the credit/charge card company immediately.

Before you start filling out a bunch of applications trying to establish credit, keep in mind that credit is a financial service, and it's your job to find the best deals available. Whether or not a credit/charge card company, bank, or financial institution accepts your application and offers you credit is dependent on many things. If you get rejected after applying for one or two credit/charge cards, don't keep submitting applications for other cards until you discover exactly why you're being denied credit and can remedy the situation.

When you're shopping around for the best deals when it comes to credit cards, keep in mind that many cards don't charge annual fees and that interest rates can vary greatly. Look for low Annual Percentage Rates (APRs). Also, read the application carefully to determine if a grace period is offered and what type of finance charges you will receive for various transactions and services.

Visa, MasterCard, American Express, Discover, and Diners Club are the most popular charge and credit cards. Many banks and credit unions offer Visa and MasterCard. You can also obtain department store credit and credit cards from gas stations. For someone first setting out to obtain credit, department store cards and charge cards are often easier to obtain.

Likewise, look for special credit/charge card applications specifically for college students. Many credit card companies, banks, and financial institutions,

including American Express, offer credit to college students, but it's necessary to fill out and submit a special application. (These applications are often distributed on college campuses.) Companies that target college students with special credit offers often include various types of incentives, such as discounted travel. American Express Green Card provides its members with dozens of benefits, including emergency road service, travel insurance, travelers checks with no fees, a full service-travel agency, and much more. As the ads say, "Membership has its privileges."

For college students, American Express offers additional special services and offers that are included in the American Express Green Card's $55 annual membership fee. This card has no preset spending limit and no interest charges, but you must pay your bill in full at the end of each month.

College students who apply for an receive the American Express Green Card receive two travel coupons per year that are good for air travel within the continental United States, on Continental Airlines, for either $159 or $239 per round-trip ticket, depending on your destination. Thirty minutes per month of free MCI long distance service is also provided for a year. This is in addition to all of American Express's other member services. Your $55 annual membership fee will quickly pay for itself the first time you use one of the travel coupons. This travel offer alone makes the American Express card an excellent deal for most college students.

American Express also offers a traditional credit card to students, which includes the travel and long distance telephone benefits. The Optima card has no annual fee; however, there is a preset spending limit and interest charges apply to all outstanding balances. In order to receive the special student benefits, it is necessary to call (800) 942-2639 during normal business hours to apply for either the American Express Green Card or the Optima card, or complete a specially marked application, which you can find on most college campuses.

In today's society, credit and charge cards offer a convenient way of paying for goods and services, but they also have become something of a necessity. For example, it's extremely difficult to rent a car or hotel room without a credit card. Also, even if you want to pay for a purchase using a personal check, you often have to show a drivers license and a major credit card for personal identification. If you're a college student, your best bet is to establish your credit history by applying for and obtaining just one credit or charge card and using it responsibly for at least one or two years. Before doing anything that involves credit, however, make sure you understand exactly what you're getting into and how to use your newly established credit. Get your questions answered by speaking with bank representatives, financial institutions, or the credit/charge card companies directly. Don't be afraid to ask questions, because while using a charge card may seem extremely simple, misusing a charge card due to lack of understanding can easily lead to personal financial and credit problems.

All banks offer Visa and MasterCard credit cards to their customers, but for the best deals in credit cards, you have to shop around. In addition to banks, many companies, clubs, retail stores, associations, professional sports teams, and major airlines offer what are called affinity credit cards. These are Visa or MasterCards that work as regular credit cards, but also come with special benefits or discounts provided by the group issuing the card in conjunction with the bank or financial institution.

When shopping for the best credit card deal, you ideally want to find a card with no annual fee and a low interest rate. Unfortunately, some of the affinity credit cards that have the best offers also have an annual fee and a slightly higher interest rate, but the benefits could be worth the extra charges. You can take full advantage of these offers, but you can avoid paying high interest fees and related charges by maintaining a low outstanding balance, and by paying your bills in a timely manner.

All of the major airlines, including American Airlines, Delta, and USAir, offer credit cards that allow you to earn frequent flier miles for every dollar you spend making regular credit card purchases. Banks and financial institutions, including MBNA, NationsBank, and American Express, offer affinity cards through the airlines. The majority of these Visa or MasterCards from the air-

lines have an annual fee. If you know you're going to be making some large purchases, such as a new computer, a Spring Break trip, or even paying your college tuition by credit card, you can earn a lot of frequent flier miles simply by putting your charges on one of these cards.

If you enjoy reading, Waldenbooks offers a special Visa card that allows you to earn points that can be applied toward earning free books. Many clothing stores offer affinity Visa or MasterCards that allow you to make purchases and earn money or points toward free clothing at their store. General Motors and Ford both offer credit cards that allow you to save hundreds or thousands of dollars on the purchase of a new GM or Ford car or pickup truck. For information about the GM Visa card, call (800) 461-3279. Be sure to ask about the special student offers.

Gas station chains, like Gulf and Mobile, also offer affinity credit cards that allow you to earn free gasoline for your car by making purchases with their Visa or MasterCard. Even companies like America On-line, the Official Star Trek Fan Club, Toys "Я" Us, and the Sharper Image offer Visa or MasterCards that have special offers for cardholders.

As you explore credit card opportunities, always read the fine print on the application carefully. Will the low advertised interest rate increase after the first six months or one year? Does the interest rate advertised apply to purchases, cash advances, and/or balances transferred from other credit cards? Is there an annual fee for the card? Some cards have no annual fees ever; others waive the annual fee for only the first six months or the first year. Are the benefits offered to card members all free of charge, or will there be additional charges for some of the benefits? Once you receive your credit card, use it responsibly. Never give your credit card number over the phone to a stranger, unless you initiated the call to place an order for a specific product or service. In other words, if someone calls you and asks for your credit card number, hang up! Likewise, when making a purchase on-line, never provide your credit card information unless you are sure that you are connected to a secure Web site. If you lose your card or believe that an unauthorized person has obtained

access to your account information, call the credit card company immediately. All credit card companies offer a toll-free phone number for reporting lost or stolen cards.

To find the best affinity card offers, check with your favorite airlines and visit your favorite stores. If an affinity card is offered through a club or association, ask to receive promotional materials from that organization. You can also call the new applications department at banks like MBNA (800-789-6701) and NationsBank (800-732-9194), both of which offer many affinity cards.

CHAPTER

5

GETTING ORGANIZED

FRESHMEN SCHEDULING SECRETS

Scheduling
Secrets

Okay, what's the difference between a straight-A student and a C student in college? In most cases the only difference between these two types of students is how well organized they are. That's right! C students can often become A students (or at least B students) simply by learning a few basic time-management and organizational skills.

Day-Timers, Inc., the company that manufactures those daily planners that millions of successful business people use to keep themselves organized, recently did a study among high school seniors and found that 65 percent of high school seniors always or frequently feel rushed to do things they need to do. Even though most people feel like there isn't enough time in the day to attend classes, do their studying, have a social life, and participate in extracurricular activities, they do little or nothing to remedy the situation.

If you simply spend a few minutes every morning making a list of everything you need to accomplish, and then organize that list by prioritizing each task and placing the things that absolutely have to be accomplished that day on the top of your list, you'll find your objectives for each day will be more focused. By referring to your list, you'll know exactly what has to be accomplished,

and you can set aside specific amounts of time during the day to accomplish those tasks. This sounds pretty simple, right? Doing this once in a while probably won't do you too much good. But if you make a habit of spending fifteen minutes every morning (or every night before you go to bed) determining exactly what you have to do, along with how and when you plan to go about doing it, you'll be well on your way to becoming a more organized person.

Over the years, Day-Timers has developed a time-management course that it calls 4-Dimensional Time Management. This course is taught to executives and business people. However, much of the information can easily be applied by college students, like you, who need to get themselves more organized. According to this time-management process, there are four primary steps you need to take in order to get yourself organized:

- **Focus**. Begin by focusing on what's really important (studying for an exam, finishing a research paper, etc.). Make a list of everything you have to get done.
- **Plan**. Prioritize your "to-do" list, placing the most critical items at the top of the list. You can use a "1-2-3" method for setting pri-

orities. Place a *1* next to items that *must* be done as soon as possible (i.e., that day). Place a *2* next to items that need to be done soon (within the next two or three days), and a *3* next to items that should be done, but that can wait up to a week, if necessary. As you make your plan, develop goals by determining what needs to be done. Next, determine a specific number, value, or amount that relates to your goal (for example, spend three hours studying for a history exam, write the first 5 pages of a research paper, read 50 pages of the textbook, etc.). Finally, set a specific deadline or time limit for accomplishing each task.

o **Act**. Determine what it will take to accomplish each item on your list, starting with the most important tasks, and then begin working on those tasks in an orderly manner. To determine what you need to do first to complete the items you have categorized as critical, ask yourself, What activities lead to achievement of your highest priority items? What projects or activities produce the highest return on your investment of time? What will happen if you do not complete the activity today? And finally, If you could only accomplish your first two items today, which would they be?'

o **Team-Up**. Maximize your success through the power of synergy. If you're working on a group project, for example, divide up the work that has to be done, based on each team member's talents. If you're participating in a study group, divide up the material that needs to be mastered, and have each person create outlines and study sheets for their portion of the material. When you work as a team or in a group, make sure that everyone you work with has a common goal or focus. Communicate your goals, priorities, and plans. Finally, collaborate to achieve success in individual and team efforts.

For well under $25, Day-Timers, Inc., offers what it calls the Day-Timer Student Planner. If you're a college student (or about to be one), this product could very well become one of the most valuable tools for achieving success in school. This product was designed by time-management professionals to help students, just like you, take control of their time so they can study smarter. This isn't just a calendar that allows you to schedule appointments and homework assignments. The Day-Timer Student Planner is a complete time-management and organizational system.

Inside the planner you'll find:

- o Two-page monthly calendars
- o Weekly dated pages
- o Class schedule sheets
- o Monthly planning sheets and assessments
- o Monthly success messages
- o Project planning forms
- o Grade-tracking sheets
- o Reference sheets and study tips
- o A notepad
- o Complete directions for putting this system to use

The Day-Timer Student Planner provides you with just about everything you'll need in one handy package that you can take with you to classes. The monthly pages are designed so that you can develop an overall plan for each month. You can use these pages to write down your long-term goals and other important events that you have to remember. These pages should be used

as a general to-do list of tasks that don't have a specific deadline.

In terms of your day-to-day planning and organization, you should use the weekly dated pages. That way, you learn to structure your time in terms of an entire week. Use these pages to write down specific appointments, assignment due dates, meetings, sports practice schedules, play rehearsal dates, and dates of parties and other social engagements. Start every week with a plan. Determine exactly what you need to get done that week by looking at your monthly pages and your class syllabi and assignment sheets. Then create a detailed plan of attack for your weekly dated pages. List the items and tasks in each day's to-do list and assignments sections.

As you go through your college years, you'll be required to meet many

different deadlines for completing class projects, papers, and presentations. For these long-term projects (which often represent a substantial part of your overall grade for a class), you can use the project planning sheets provided with the student planner to help you keep track of the details pertaining to each project. These project sheets will also help to keep you on schedule, because they require you to break up a large project into smaller tasks.

For example, if you have a twenty-page research paper due in thirty days, instead of worrying about how you can possibly get this project completed, you can break it down into smaller, more manageable tasks, which the project sheets refer to as key milestones. Here are some

potential key milestones you'll need to deal with when writing a research paper:

○ Think of a topic for your paper.
○ Determine the key points you need to make in your paper. (Write them down.)
○ Determine what research materials you will need to write this paper. (Make a list.)
○ Determine what research materials you already have, and what you'll have to locate at a library or on-line?

- Create an outline for the paper. Break up the overall topic into sections.
- Gather your research materials (keeping careful notes for your bibliography).
- Perform the needed research.
- Write the first draft of your paper.
- Write the second draft (if needed) of your paper.
- Proofread and edit your paper.
- Desktop publish your paper using your computer (or a computer at your school's computer center). Make the paper looks professional.

Whether or not you choose to use the Day-Timer Student Planner, it is critical that you use some type of written planner/calendar to keep track of your school work and other obligations. Whenever you attend classes, do research in the library, attend group meetings, and so forth, always have your planner and a pen with you, so you can make notes to yourself or add appointments to your schedule. The biggest mistake you can make is to keep dozens of small pieces of scrap paper containing important homework assignments and appointments in your pocket, on your dresser, and stuck in your various notebooks.

Use a planner to keep all of these notes in one place, where you can refer to them easily.

Remember, to get yourself truly organized, you should spend between ten and fifteen minutes every morning planning your upcoming day. Enter into your calendar all scheduled events. Create and prioritize a detailed "action list" for that day. Keep a running record of each day's events and important information. And at the end of each day, check off everything that you accomplished, and make notes to yourself about items that need to be completed the following day.

One thing you should do to make sure that you're always on time for meetings, classes, and appointments is wear a wristwatch. Learning how to manage your time now, while in college, will not only help you boost your grades but also help you once you graduate and begin your career.

For more information about the Day-Timer Student Planner, call (800) 225-5005.

Take an Electronic Approach to Organization

Instead of keeping track of your life with a paper and pen, you can take a more high-tech approach. There are many scheduling programs available for personal computers that are ideal for business people who work at a desk or from an office. But as a college student, you're going to be spending a lot of time on the go. Having to run back to your computer every time you need to write down an appointment or refer to your schedule probably isn't the best approach to take.

The alternative is to use a personal digital assistant (PDA). These handheld, electronic devices cost anywhere from $49 to $1,000+, and are actually specialized computers. The simplest and least expensive PDAs can be used to keep track of appointments, phone numbers, addresses, important dates (birthdays, etc.), to-do lists, and other types of short notes. The more expensive PDAs also have built-in spreadsheets, calculators, word processors (or text editors), and even fax machines and modems.

What's nice about these PDAs is that they often fit in your pocket, back-pack, or purse, and they can hold large amounts of information that can be organized and customized to meet your personal needs. Some of the manufacturers of PDAs include Sharp (which offers a line of electronic organizers called Wizards), Casio, Hewlett Packard, Apple, and Psion. If you go to an office supply store, such as Staples or Office Max, or an electronics store, you'll find many of these PDAs on display. Look for one that has the features you think you'll need. As a college student, the most important features to look for are a good scheduling program, a powerful calculator, and an electronic to-do-list manager. If you're studying a foreign language, some of these PDAs also offer add-ons, such as translators, that could come in handy. If you're a finance or accounting major, having a spreadsheet program that's compatible with Lotus 1-2-3 and/or Microsoft Excel might come in handy. What's great about the more expensive PDAs is that you can transfer data between the PDA and a PC using an optional cable.

Organize More Than Your Time

Chances are you're going to be taking a number of courses each semester. To help stay organized, at the start of each semester, purchase a separate loose-leaf binder for each course. In this binder, keep plenty of paper (for taking notes), along with several folders (to keep papers from falling out). Inside the folders, keep handouts, test papers, or other pieces of loose paper that are related to that course.

Label each binder with the name of the subject/course and be sure to place your name, address, and phone number both on the inside and the outside of each binder (in case it gets lost). Near the front of your binder, where you can access it easily, place your syllabus for that class. You should also write down your professor's name, office location, telephone number, and office hours. Also, make a list of several people in each of your classes, and write their names and phone numbers inside of the binder. That way, if you happen to miss a class (since, in college, attendance isn't always mandatory, and sometimes parties go a little to late into the night making it tough to wake up in the morning for classes), you'll have a list of people to call in order to get notes and homework assignments.

Bring your binder to every class, and take all of your notes on the pages of the binder. At the top of each page, be sure to write the date of the class along with the topic of the days notes. This will make studying and reviewing for exams much easier.

Any homework assignments that the professor assigns should be listed on the syllabus for the class, which you should copy into your planner. Also, if the professor adds assignments or modifies them, be sure to write this information both in your binder for that class and in your planner.

For additional tips on how to use your newfound organizational skills to earn good grades, be sure to read the sections of this book that deal with the following subjects:

- Developing good study habits
- Preparing for final exams, midterm exams, and finals
- Getting A's
- Using the library
- Doing research on-line
- Writing papers

CHAPTER 6

COMPUTERS
A COLLEGE STUDENT'S BEST FRIEND

Yo, in case you haven't noticed, this is your wake-up call! The world is in the midst of a computer revolution, and getting a good job may ultimately depend on how comfortable you are working with computers. A computer will also prove to be an extremely useful tool while you're in school. In fact, most colleges and universities now require that all incoming students own (or at least have access to) a personal computer. Most professors require students to submit all of their research papers and homework assignments on laser-printed output. And just about all colleges are now connected to the Internet.

What does this mean to you? Well, for starters, you'd better get yourself up to speed, and learn to use a personal computer . . . fast. Ideally, you should begin your freshman year of college with a working knowledge of computers—not how to program them, but a general knowledge of word processing, how to use a spreadsheet, and how to connect to a major on-line service and/or the Internet. If your high school education didn't include teaching you these critical skills, find an introductory computer class that's being taught in your city (such as at a local computer store) and sign up for it. As a last resort, register to take an introduction to computers class

(Computers 101) during your first semester of college. (A class will also enable you to learn the buzzwords that'll help you buy the best system to meet your needs.)

Buying a computer for school can be confusing if you're not computer literate. Most schools recommend to incoming students either a PC- or Macintosh-based system. If your school recommends a specific computer system, go with that recommendation. Some schools even sell computer systems to students at large discounts. This can save you some serious cash. If you're instructed to purchase your own computer system, this chapter offers some general guidelines to follow.

Begin by choosing a PC-based computer (a computer that is 100 percent IBM compatible), or an Apple Macintosh-based system. Macs are easier to use but are not supported by many schools. Furthermore, most companies and businesses use PC-based computers, so when you graduate, you might want to have a strong knowledge of PC-based computers (that can run under Windows 95 or Microsoft's latest operating system.) If you choose to purchase a PC-based computer, you must determine if you want a desktop computer or a laptop computer. Obviously, a desktop computer is large, and it must be plugged in and kept on a desk or tabletop. A laptop, however, is smaller, portable, and battery powered (or can be plugged into an electrical outlet).

Both desktop and laptop computers now offer the same computing power; however, desktop computers tend to be cheaper. Again, if your school recommends that you purchase a laptop, go with that recommendation. Some courses may require you to bring your laptop to class in order to complete assignments. Having a computer with you in the library while doing research can also help you save time.

There are two components to a computer system: the hardware and the software. In terms of the hardware, you want to purchase the most powerful system that you can afford. Keep in mind that technology changes quickly, so choose a system that will work for you now, understanding that by the time you graduate, it will probably be outdated technology. The following is a recommended list of PC-based system requirements that will be suitable for almost every college student's needs:

- You want a Pentium-based microprocessor. Pentium chips come in several speeds. You want your computer to have the highest speed microprocessor that you can afford. For desktop computers, a Pentium 120 (or better) is recommended. To save money, especially if you're purchasing a laptop computer, you can go with a slower speed Pentium-based processor, but avoid a 386 or 486 processor, since these processors have become outdated technology.

- Memory is another important component of your computer hardware. Make sure your PC-based computer system has at least 16 megabytes of RAM memory (more is better).

- The computer's hard disk is where you'll be storing all of your programs and data. Once again, you want to purchase the largest hard disk you can afford—a minimum of 800-meg is recommended.

- A computer's disk drive is also important. A computer should have at least one 1.44 Mb 3.5-inch built-in disk drive. A CD-Rom drive is also becoming increasingly more important, and is required to run virtually all multimedia software. If you're purchasing a desktop computer, it should have at least a 4x speed CD-Rom drive installed. For a laptop computer, you can get either a CD-Rom drive that's built-in (which costs more money), or an external CD-Rom drive (which is sold separately.)

○ The computer's display type is what allows you to see what you're doing on the screen. Full-sized computer monitors range in price. Make sure that your monitor is Super VGA compatible. For laptop users, you want a laptop with a color LCD display (that's also Super VGA compatible). Passive LCD displays are cheaper, but the quality isn't as good as an active color LCD display. If you're going with a cheaper laptop display, you might consider getting an external color monitor, so make sure your laptop has a port for connecting an external monitor (most of them do).

○ A computer printer is what you'll use to generate hard copy (paper printouts) of your work. A 600 dots-per-inch laser printer is best suited for your needs, but even personal laser printers can be a bit expensive. Again, go with the best you can afford. A nice (and less expensive) alternative to a laser printer is an ink-jet printer. When choosing a printer, the two main things to look for are the resolution (measured in dots-per-

inch) and the number of pages the printer can print per minute. For resolution, don't settle for anything less than 300 dpi. In terms of speed, you want to purchase the printer with the fastest print speed you can afford. When you visit a computer store, ask to see sample printouts from the printers that the salesperson recommends to you.

○ The customer service and technical support that's offered by the computer manufacturer and the retail store or mail order company you choose is also something that's definitely worth considering. Choose a company that offers a technical support phone number that's available twenty-four hours per day, seven days per week. You also want to insure that the computer you choose will be easily repairable should something go wrong. These are the types of questions you should get answers to before making an investment in a specific computer system: What is the repair policy and how long does the warranty period last? Can you purchase a longer warranty? If something goes wrong, can you bring the computer back to the dealer, or do you have to ship it back to the manufacturer? If you have to ship it back for repair, who pays for the shipping, and how long will it take to fix?

When choosing a computer system, visit one or two computer stores (or superstores), and have the salesperson demonstrate several different systems to you. If you're not too familiar with computers, choose a computer system that comes preassembled, with all of the hardware and a selection of software already set up. For example, IBM offers the Aptiva line and Compaq offers the popular (and powerful) Presario line of PC-based personal computers. If you decide to go with an Apple Macintosh-based computer system or an Apple PowerBook laptop, visit an authorized Apple computer dealer to learn about your options.

Once you know exactly what type of computer and system configuration you're looking for, you can purchase it from a retail store, or you can often save money by purchasing your system via mail order. Publications like *Computer Shopper* offer page after page of ads that list good deals. If you

buy your computer via mail order, make sure that the company is reputable and use a major credit card to pay for the system.

A modem is a device that allows your computer to communicate with other computers via the telephone lines. A modem can be internal (it fits inside your computer), external (it's located in a separate box that is connected to your computer), or in the form of a PCMCIA card (a credit-card-sized device that fits into the special socket found in many laptop or portable computers). Most computers sold these days come equipped with a modem. However, you should make sure that your modem is the right speed. Modems communicate with other computers by sending information back and forth at predefined speeds called baud rates. The most popular modem baud rates are 14.4, 28.8, 33.6, and 57.6. In general, the faster the modem is able to communicate, the higher the cost of the modem. If you're planning to surf the Web or hang out on an on-line service, like America On-line, you'll need at least a 28.8 modem. (The higher the modem's speed, the better!)

When purchasing a new PC-based computer, you'll quickly discover that many hardware companies offer large selections of computer models that range in price and capabilities. These manufacturers are divided into two main categories: name brand computers (IBM, Compaq, etc.) and clone computers. Clones offer the same power and capabilities, but often cost less. Yes, you can save money by purchasing a computer from a clone manufacturer, especially if you purchase it by mail, but the customer service and the ability to get your computer repaired quickly and easily may be difficult. For someone first learning about computers, it's an excellent idea to spend a bit more money and purchase your computer from a well-established computer store that you can return to if problems or questions arise as you use your computer.

Once you have your computer, you're going to need software. Most PC-based computers these days come with the Microsoft Windows 95 operating system. If your computer doesn't come with this operating system, consider upgrading, especially if it's the operating system your school recommends. As a college student, three software applications you're definitely going to need are a word processor, spreadsheet, and telecommunications (used for con-

necting to the Internet). Once again, go with the software that your school recommends, or stick with the most popular software on the market. For a word processor, Microsoft Word is an excellent choice, and for a spreadsheet, both Microsoft Excel and Lotus 1-2-3 offer equal power. Microsoft offers a package called the Microsoft Office, which includes Word and Excel, along with several other useful applications, all in one package.

As for the software needed to link up your computer to your school's computer system and to the Internet, chances are that your school will supply it. In addition, you should consider joining one of the major on-line services, such as America On-line, The Microsoft Network, or CompuServe, because these services allow you to perform research on virtually any topic on-line, which can save you countless hours spent in the library.

Your computer will become a valuable tool while you're in school, and the more you know about how to use it, the better off you'll be. Take a computer class, read computer books, ask friends to teach you, and spend time at your school's computer center. Do whatever it takes to get yourself totally comfortable with using your computer in all of your courses.

CHAPTER

7

CHOOSING YOUR CLASSES AND YOUR MAJOR

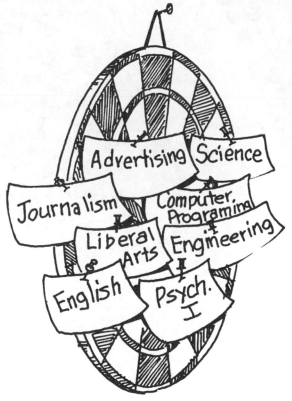

Okay, you get to school and within the very first days, you must choose your first semester classes. You don't know any of the professors, you're not familiar with any of the classes, and you really have no clue about what to choose for your major. Welcome to your first year at college! EVERYONE is in exactly the same position. It's absolutely nothing to worry about.

The good news is that just about every college or university requires all incoming freshmen to take a predetermined number of required classes (which vary depending on the school.) You're biggest challenge is deciding the order in which you want to take these required classes, and then choosing your professors (assuming multiple professors teach the same course). You have to fit these classes into your overall schedule. So when the classes are taught (the days of the week and the times) will be a determining factor regarding which classes you select. When it comes to class registration, seniors, juniors, and sophomores are given first choice. As a result, when it's time for you to register, you may find that your first choices for classes are already filled; so have a second (and a third) choice ready before you go to register.

When choosing your classes, here are a few things to consider:

○ Read the course descriptions for each of the required classes you'll have to take during your first (and most likely your sophomore) year. Think about which of these classes you think you'll enjoy, and the ones you know you'll hate. Next, think about which of the required classes will be easy for you to earn a good grade in, and which of the classes you think will be the most challenging. Based on these decisions, take one or two that you know you're going to love (and that will be relatively easy for you) and one or two that will require more work and don't necessarily interest you.

○ Once you pinpoint the classes you think will be the most difficult for you personally, spread them out over the first few semesters you're at school. In any one semester, you shouldn't overwhelm yourself with too many difficult courses, or more than two or three courses that require a lot of reading.

○ Are you a morning person? If you can't wait to jump out of bed bright and early every morning, and you think that you're the most alert during the morning hours, then you are a morning person. Thus, you should attempt to schedule your classes for the morning. If you know you won't be able to get yourself out of bed and get yourself to class by 8:00 or 9:00 a.m., then be sure to sign up for mid-morning or after-noon classes. As a freshman, you'll find that attendance is mandatory for the majority of your classes, so plan on showing up for every class, even if you were up late studying or partying the night before.

○ Make sure you sign up for at least one or two classes each semester that will be fun and that really interest you. At the same time, make an effort to get all of your required classes done as

PROFESSORS COUNT MORE THAN YOU THINK

When it comes time to choosing a professor, listen to what other students have to say, plus take the time to read the student evaluation forms for each faculty member. This information is often available at your school library. Warning: Information about a professor passed by word of mouth, especially if it's negative, isn't always an honest evaluation. If you hear that a certain professor is, for example, very mean, extremely difficult, or very boring, do some additional research. Remember, virtually every school allows you to sit in on a class, and, if you choose, change professors/classes within the first few days of each semesters. Your class decisions during registration aren't 100 percent final. If you happen to make a bad decision, and you know that you're not going to get along with a certain professor, switch out of that class during the first two or three classes. One way you can evaluate a professor firsthand is to drop by his or her office before registration. Introduce yourself and explain that you're about to sign up for his or her classes. This gives you a chance to meet the professor before you actually make a commitment.

If you keep hearing about how wonderful a certain professor is, consider signing up for that person's class. Introduction to English Literature or Accounting 101 (both of which are often required classes) can be taught in an exciting and interesting way; or they can be the most boring classes you'll be forced to sit through. It all depends on the quality of the professor teaching the course.

quickly as you can, so you can move on to more advanced and exciting courses.

○ As an incoming freshmen, don't be too concerned about choosing your major. This is something you can do a bit later. Right now, your main concern should be to get your required courses out of the way, and to get yourself acclimated to your new school.

○ Many schools provide each incoming student with a faculty advisor. If you have any questions about specific classes or faculty members, or you need help choosing classes, your advisor can be extremely helpful, so seek out his or her advice. If you don't get the answers you need from your faculty advisor, or if you run into some type of problem with a professor, make an appointment to see a Dean.

○ The class registration process can be a bit overwhelming and even scary for incoming freshmen. Relax . . . don't panic. Your best bet is to go to registration fully prepared. Make sure all of your bills have been paid (the school won't let you register otherwise), and that you have preselected the classes you're interested in taking. Have second and third choices

ready in case a class you wanted is already filled. Before registration, you will be told what paperwork you must bring with you and what forms need to be filled out in advance. Make sure you have everything you'll need with you.

○ Obviously, your class schedule takes priority. However, as you're choosing classes and fitting them into your schedule, think about the time requirements of extracurricular activities you may be interested in. Will you be participating in sports and need specific times available for practices? If you'll be involved in the school's drama department, when will rehearsals be? Or do you need afternoons free for a part-time job? Before registration, it's an excellent strategy to use a calendar, time chart, or daily planner (such as the Day-Timer Student Planner) to lay out your overall schedule on paper. As you plan each day's class schedule, don't forget to leave yourself time for lunch. Also, if possible, avoid signing up for two or more lecture-based classes in a row. After all, you'll do much better if you're able to stay awake and alert for each of your classes. Sitting through three or more hours of nonstop lectures can get boring.

Choosing a Major

Your choice of college or university is already a first step toward choosing your major, because every school has a unique atmosphere and curriculum that caters to certain interests. As a freshman, you can start thinking about a major, but before you choose take this time to sample many different types of courses in a variety of subject areas. When it comes time to actually declaring your major, you want to have a good general knowledge of the types of subject areas that are available to you.

If you're hoping to be a doctor or follow some very structured education path that will lead to a specific career, you might have to declare your major early. Otherwise, think of your first year as a time to expose yourself to new subject areas and experiences.

Declaring your major is the first step toward determining a career path, so give this plenty of thought. Many people wind up in jobs that have absolutely nothing to do with their major, so your decision is not totally binding. You can also switch majors or declare a double major if your interests change as you proceed with your education.

As you think about a major, consider what really interests you. What do you love doing? What are your personal skills and strengths? What weaknesses will you have to overcome? Most importantly, whatever major you choose, make sure that it's something you truly love. Having a passion for whatever it is that you wind up doing will automatically give you a huge advantage toward ultimately being successful.

CHAPTER **8**

TRAVELING TO SCHOOL
GETTING THERE IS HALF THE FUN

f you're attending school away from your hometown, getting to and from home and school will mean having to travel. The cheapest way to get from one place to another is to take a car, bus, or train (call Greyhound Bus at [800] 231-2222 or Amtrak at [800] USA-RAIL). These methods of transportation will save you money, but they take longer and are less comfortable than flying. Should you have to embark on a long car, bus, or train trip, plan accordingly. Bring along books, magazines, a Walkman, schoolwork, snack foods, and drinks. Also, when booking your travel arrangements, ask about promotional fares and specials. Before kicking off a long car trip, check the car's oil and tire pressure, and fill up the tank with gas. You might also want to go to a place like Midas Mufflers and have the brakes checked. Make sure you bring along maps or directions, so you don't get lost. If you're driving to someplace

you've never been, try to do your traveling during daylight hours.

Traveling by airplane to and from home and school can be a costly endeavor, but there are many ways of saving money. First, all airlines offer major discounts if you book your travel 21, 14, or even 7 days in advance. Also, many airlines offer special student rates. Always book a round-trip ticket. If necessary, you can leave the return date open (or choose a return date that can be changed, sometimes for a small fee). When booking your ticket, ask for a seat assignment. This will allow you to choose a window, center, or aisle seat. Make sure you bring along your own snacks, along with a Walkman headset (so you don't have to rent a set in order to watch the in-flight movie). Also, make sure that you arrive at the airport about one hour prior to your departure time. This will give you ample time to check your bags, get a seat assignment

(if necessary), and locate the correct departure gate.

If air travel is necessary, plan your travel as far in advance as possible to get the best rates. Next, join a frequent flier club for the airline(s) of your choice, and rack up frequent flier miles in order to earn free travel. By the time you reach your sophomore or junior year, you could have enough miles for a free trip (which will come in handy when planning your spring break vacation). To find the best rates, call the airlines directly, and also consult at least two different travel agents. Every airline has an 800 number, and travel agents are listed in the phone book.

Another way to earn free flights is to book yourself on flights that are almost always full, and then offer to give up your seat if the flight is oversold. The airlines will sometimes reward you with a free round-trip ticket, or at least a first class upgrade. When you check in at the ticket counter before your flight, ask if they are looking for volunteers to give up their seats.

If you're flying on one the busiest travel days of the year, for example, like Thanksgiving, you may have to be flexible when booking your flight. Ask the airline or travel agent if it's cheaper to fly into an alternate airport. For example, if you're flying in or out of New York, you can use Laguardia, JFK, or Newark airports. Newark is a smaller airport, and some airlines offer special promotional rates for using this airport; it is extremely convenient to New York City and surrounding areas. Just about every major U.S. city has alternate airports you can ask about. (For example, when going to or from Los Angeles, you can travel through LAX, Orange County, or Burbank airports.)

Everyone worries about taking a plane and having the airline lose their bags. Before leaving home, place luggage tags on the outside of your bags (don't use stickers that can peel off). Also, place your name, address, and phone

number on the inside of each suitcase and bag you'll be checking. When you arrive at the airport, go to the inside ticket counter and check your bags. Make sure you are given a claim check (that will often contain a number and bar code). Keep your claim check safe in your wallet or with your airline ticket. If the airline happens to lose your luggage, immediately report it to the airline's baggage claims desk (located near the baggage-claim area of every airport.) Be sure that you can describe what your luggage looks like in detail (color, size, and manufacturer), and be prepared to present your claim stubs.

If the airline can't locate your bags immediately, insist that they deliver them to your destination. This is a service they offer free of charge to make up for the delay and inconvenience. Many credit cards, such as Diners Club and American Express, offer special travelers' insurance that automatically kicks in if you purchase your airline ticket using that credit card. Thus, if your bags do get lost, even for a few hours, you're entitled to financial compensation from the credit card company as well as from the airline. Also, American Express offers special travel deals for student members. Contact American Express for details.

Warning: Always pack your own luggage. And never volunteer to carry a suitcase, handbag, or package for a stranger.

Here are some major airline phone numbers:

Alaska Airlines	(800) 426-0333
American Airlines	(800) 433-7300
Continental	(800) 523-3273
Delta	(800) 221-1212
Northwest Airlines	(800) 225-2525
MidWest Express	(800) 452-2022
TWA	(800) 221-2000
United	(800) 241-6522
USAir	(800) 428-4322

CHAPTER

9

EXPLORING TERRITORY
SETTING UP IN A NEW CITY

I f you're one of the millions of students who is going away to school, one of the challenges early in your college experience will be getting to know your way around. One of the first things you need to do is find out what your mailing address will be at school. After obtaining this information, send Change of Address cards (available at your local U.S. Post Office) to any daily or weekly newspapers or magazine that you subscribe to. Or you could continue to have them delivered to your home and then pick them up when you return for a visit, or have your parents send them to you. Also distribute your new address to your friends.

Setting Up Phone Service

Ask your school about phone service. You may be responsible for contacting the local telephone company and arranging for it yourself. As soon as you know your exact address (including your dorm room number), you can contact the local phone company and arrange to have your new phone number activated once you arrive at school. Don't have phone service activated before you arrive! Some schools have their own telephone systems, which means you won't have to contact the phone company. Your school's housing office will be able to provide you with the information necessary for establishing phone service in your dorm room.

With a telephone comes the phone bills. As soon as phone service is established, you'll be able to call anywhere in the world, but each time you dial the phone to make a long distance call, it's going to cost money. If you know you'll be making long distance calls, choose a long distance phone company that offers the best deals. For example, Sprint offers a ten cents per minute rate, but only during certain hours. To save money, sign up for one of these special rates, and then make your calls only during the designated times when the rates are low. There are now dozens of long distance telephone companies. Each offers special promotions and discount rates. Here are some of the long distance phone companies you can call:

AT&T	(800) 222-3000
Sprint	(800) 877-4646
MCI	(800) 950-5555
Dime Line	
(VarTel Telecom)	(800) 583-5803
LDDS Worldcom	(800) 570-0286

Special phone services, such as Touch Tone, Call Waiting, and Caller ID, are provided by your local phone company for an additional monthly fee. Here's a quick rundown of the popular phone services that most phone companies now offer. Unfortunately, not all of these services are available in all towns and cities; contact your local phone company for availability and pricing.

- *Touch Tone Service.* In the olden days (less than 10 years ago), rotary dial phones were standard. These phones had round dials that you had to use to dial the telephone. Rotary dial phones were replaced with Touch Tone service (instead of clicking noises, it makes those beeps when you press the buttons on the phone). In many parts of the country, Touch Tone service is now standard. To use voice mail or other automated phone services, Touch Tone service is required.
- *Three-Way Calling* (also known as Conference Calling or Circle Calling). This service allows you to call someone on the phone or receive a call, put that person on hold, and then call a third party into the conversation.
- *Calling Waiting.* When someone tries to call you and you're talking on the phone, unless you have Call Waiting, they'd get a busy signal. With this service, when you're on the phone and someone else tries to reach you, you'll hear a beep or click. This sound notifies you of an incoming call. You then have the option to put the original call on hold and answer the incoming call. You can then switch back and forth between calls. This service is a must for dorm rooms with two or more people and only one phone line. In some cities, before making an outgoing call, you can press *70 on a Touch Tone phone and temporarily turn off Call Waiting so you won't be disturbed during the call. Anyone who tries to call you once you have pressed *70 will receive a busy signal until you hang up. Once your call is complete, your Call Waiting service will automatically reactivate. If you're planning to use your fax machine or computer (with a modem) with your phone line, be sure to disable Call Waiting (*70) before allowing the fax machine or computer to make a call.
- *Call Answering.* Instead of buying an answering machine, Call Answering acts as an electronic voice mail service that's provided for a fee by your phone company. Call Answering works just like an answering machine, except to record your outgoing message or to hear your incoming messages, you pick up the phone and dial a special code. You can also retrieve your messages from any Touch Tone phone or pay phone. The benefit to Call Answering is that you can never run out of tape on your answering machine, and you don't have to worry about power failures in your dorm or apartment, which would cause your answering machine to stop working. Another benefit is that Call Answering can be used in conjunction with Call Waiting. If you're on the phone and you receive another call, you can choose to not answer the incoming call and the caller will automatically be passed over to your Call Answering service so they can leave a message.

- *Caller ID.* To use this service, you either need a Caller ID box connected to your telephone or you need a phone that's compatible with this service. What Caller ID does is display the telephone number of the person calling you, so you know who is calling before you pick up the phone. Caller ID lets you screen your incoming calls, so you can avoid people you don't want to talk to. Caller ID can work with Call Waiting in most areas.
- **69.* Were you ever unable to answer a call because you were in the shower or couldn't get to the phone before the person calling hung up? With the *69 service, after you miss a call, all you have to do is dial *69 on a Touch Tone phone, and you will be connected to the person who just called you. There is a charge for using *69, plus you are billed for making the call to the person who just hung up.
- **66.* If you receive a busy signal and don't feel like redialing a number multiple times until the line is available, you can dial *66 when you first hear the busy signal and then hang up. Your phone will automatically monitor the number you're trying to reach for up to 30 minutes. When the number you are trying to reach is clear, your phone will ring (using a special ring that sounds different from the usual ring). When you pick up the phone, the number will be automatically dialed. There is a charge each time you use this service. Consult your phone company for details.
- *Call Forwarding.* This service allows you to have all of your incoming calls forwarded to another phone number. If you don't have an answering machine or Call Answering, you can have your calls ring at any phone number you enter. So, for example, if you're at a friend's house, people can reach you there by dialing your regular phone number. You can also use Call Forwarding to send your incoming calls to a cellular phone or beeper. In addition to the monthly service fee for Call Forwarding, you are billed any long distance phone charges that apply for having your calls forwarded to another number. The person calling you is not aware that you have forwarded their call to another number.
- *Ring Mate.* Here's another service that can be useful to a group of people living in a dorm room or apartment with only one phone line. With Ring Mate, your one phone can be given up to four different phone numbers—one for each person living with you. Each number will have a different ring, so each person will know who the incoming call is for.
- *Speed Calling.* If there are a number of phone numbers that you dial often, Speed Dialing allows you to enter these numbers into your phone once, and associate them with a one- or two-digit number. So, for example, if you wanted to call your parents, you'd simply press 1, or to call your boyfriend/girlfriend, you'd dial 2 instead of the complete seven or ten digit phone number.

Your local phone company is always working to improve service by offering new features. Check with your phone company to learn about additional features and services offered.

Special phone services are also available in most areas. Touch Tone, Three-Way-Calling, Call Waiting, Call Answering, and Caller ID are just some of the additional services offered by most telephone companies. There is an additional monthly charge for each of the extra services you choose to have activated. If you're in a living arrangement that includes one or more roommates, consider having Call Waiting added to your service.

As soon as your phone service is established, work out with your roommate how you will pay the bill. Your phone bill will most likely consist of general service charges (for local service, local calls, optional services, etc.) and your long distance phone charges. Everyone who uses the phone should be responsible for paying for their own long distance calls. When you establish your phone service, set up the account in everyone's name. If the account is in your name and your roommate racks up huge phone bills that he/she can't afford to pay, guess who's responsible? That's right, you! The same is true for utility bills, such as gas and electricity, if your school makes you establish accounts directly with these utilities.

Learn Where Things Are and How to Get to Them

Before leaving for school, spend some time doing a bit of research about the city and state where your school is located. If you'll be going to school in a major city, like New York, Los Angeles, San Francisco, Chicago, or Boston, pick up a travel guide for that city at your local bookstore. A travel guide for a specific city will contain useful background information, maps, and other details about the area you'll be living in.

Once you actually arrive at school, some of the things you'll want to locate and learn about in your area include:

○ Main roads (learn to find your way around campus and town)
○ Public transportation (directions to and from the train station, bus station, and/or airport)
○ Crime areas (places to avoid)
○ Restaurants (find out which local eating places deliver!)

○ Banks
○ Post office
○ Gas stations
○ Convenience stores, supermarkets, and pharmacies
○ Shopping center or mall
○ Cab/taxi companies
○ Hot spots (nightclubs, movie theaters, comedy clubs, hang outs, etc.)
○ Hair stylist/barbershop/beauty salon
○ Hospital/emergency room/medical center
○ Package (liquor) store (You should check the state law concerning the legal drinking age. As a minor, you should NEVER consider purchasing alcohol illegally, for example, by using a fake ID.)

Exploring a new city can be fun, especially if you can gather up a group of new friends to do it with. Choose a day, like the first Saturday or Sunday after you arrive at school, and spend the day exploring. Learn what bus, train, or subway routes lead to the places you want to go, and spend some time learning the public transportation system in your new city.

Personal Banking

Shortly after you arrive at school, you'll want to set up a personal checking account for yourself at a local bank. Many banks offer special student packages, for example, with no-fee checking or no minimum balance requirements, so shop around for the best deals. Ask the bank representative about services charges and other fees associated with opening and maintaining a savings/checking account.

One of the most important things you should consider is the quantity and locations of ATM machines that the bank you choose offers. If you want to have immediate and easy access to your money, ATMs offer this twenty-four hours per day. Make sure your bank is associated with a network, such as Cirrus or NYCE. This will insure that you can use your ATM card at machines around the country. Also, check out if there are service charges associated with using the ATM. This is a new way banks can take advantage of customers. Always read the fine print.

Many banks now offer an ATM card that also acts like a Visa or MasterCard. Instead of offering you credit, when you use this card to make a purchase, the money is taken directly from your checking account. This is a handy feature, but it is not a credit card. Chances are, your bank will also offer credit cards which you'll have to apply for separately. Before doing this, look for the lowest interest rates, and make sure there is no annual fee. Refer to the credit chapter for more information on establishing credit.

After opening your checking account, it's important that you learn how to balance your checkbook (or at least keep from bouncing checks). If you have a computer, there are several personal financial packages, such as QUICKEN or MICROSOFT MONEY, that are very easy to use, and will balance your checkbook for you. Remember, bouncing checks not only gets expensive (because there are high fees you have to pay for each returned check), it's also illegal, and potentially embarrassing.

CHAPTER

10

HOME-SICKNESS

FORGET DOROTHY—THERE IS SOMEPLACE LIKE HOME

For many incoming freshmen, this is the very first time living away from home—away from friends and family. If you're in this position, you're going to experience sudden and major changes in your life, and adapting to these changes will take some getting used to. Many people experience homesickness during their first few weeks at school, but this isn't something to be ashamed of. During your first weeks and months at school, living on your own, you're going to face many new challenges. You'll have to make decisions for yourself, and then live with the outcome of those decisions. This is all part of the growing up process.

Whatever you experience during your first few weeks of college, chances are it'll be nothing like what you imagined. For some people, it'll be better, and for others, it'll be worse, or at least very different. Try to enter your first semester at school with a totally open mind, leaving home all preconceptions. This is an opportunity for you to start off fresh, make new friends, and grow as a person.

Feeling homesick or overwhelmed by your new surroundings should be expected. Looking back at how wonderful your high school years were and how popular you were isn't going to help you in your new surroundings. Think about what qualities you like about yourself the most and what it took to make

your high school friends, and then consider everything you can do to re-create that in your new situation at college.

If your feelings of homesickness become intense, don't jump to the conclusion that you're not fitting in, or that you don't belong at your new school. And whatever you do, don't let your depression affect your eating habits. It is very common for freshmen to gain weight once their first semester begins. Try to stick to a well-balanced diet and avoid the temptation of "pigging out" on junk food in between meals or in the middle of the night when you're up late studying. If you want to have a snack, make sure it's a relatively healthy one. As a freshman, you have enough to deal with already, so don't start any new diet plans, or try to starve yourself. Do little things like avoiding excessive caffeine, sugar, and fatty foods instead. Drink plenty of water instead of soda, and instead of a candy bar, eat a granola bar or a piece of fruit. Also, find some time to exercise—take a walk, jog, Rollerblade, work out at the gym, take an aerobics class, go for a swim, take a bike ride—doing whatever you enjoy that's active. This will help you manage your weight and relieve stress, and will even help to alleviate feelings of homesickness. The very worst thing you can do if you're feeling homesick or depressed is to sit in your dorm room and stare at the ceiling feeling sorry for yourself!

Give yourself time to adjust. After a semester, if you still feel like you don't belong, or that you chose the wrong school to attend, then you can consider transferring to another school. Remember, very few new students feel like they truly belong at their new school after only a few days or even a few weeks.

Even if everything is going incredibly well at school and you quickly adjust to life on your own, don't ignore your parents. Stay in touch with them on a regular basis. Call home once a week and tell them some of the highlights about what's happening in your life. You may be feeling totally grown up, but you still need your parents, and chances are, they really miss you. There will be times during your college years that you'll need advice from your parents, and there will be plenty of times when your parents feel that you need their advice even if you don't. Over time, you'll develop a balance. Also, don't blow off your old friends. Call or write to them, and plan visits. However, during your first few months of school, your focus should be on meeting new people, exploring new interests, and getting totally involved in your new surroundings. The more involved you become and the more fun you begin having, the less homesick you'll feel—guaranteed.

The trick to surviving this challenging time is to not get caught up too deeply in any problems. If any problem arises that seems too big for you to handle, don't deal with it alone. Seek help from friends, family members, school guidance counselors, faculty members, or anyone you can trust.

Every college and university has a counseling office (or student affairs office), which offers non-medical assistance to students, free of charge. Often, these offices are staffed by psychologists or other trained professionals who can help you deal with personal or school-related problems. The people working in a counseling office can help you work out problems, work as an intermediary between you and a faculty member or roommate, or provide you with a referral to someone who can help with your particular situation. Most of the time, the services provided by a counseling office are totally confidential. However, if your problem is of a highly personal nature, you might want to confirm this before spilling your guts. Anytime you just need someone to talk to, because you're feeling overwhelmed, stressed out, or depressed, you can visit the counseling office at your school. As you go through school, you will, without a doubt, be faced with some difficult situations. Seeking advice or guidance is always a smart move, and working to solve small problems before they become too big is an ideal way to insure your happiness and well-being.

STRESS

CHAPTER

STRESS

GET IT OUT OF YOUR LIFE AND MOVE ON

For some people, the quest to be a "perfect student" is a stressful experience. Combine the pressure of your studies with a busy social schedule, and stress can easily become part of your daily life. Without a bit of stress in your life, things would be pretty dull, but if you let the stress build up too much, it can be unhealthy both physically and mentally.

When stress occurs in your life, you must learn how to deal with it effectively. First, it's important that you discover what aspects of your life create the most stress and pinpoint exactly how that stress affects you.

The Consumer Information Catalog offers a free booklet called *Plain Talk About . . . Handling Stress*, which describes how you can best deal with stress. To receive this booklet, write to the Consumer Information Catalog, P.O. Box 100, Pueblo, Colorado, 81002. If you have access to the Internet, you can also download this publication from the Consumer Information Catalog's Web site (http://www.pueblo.gsa.gov).

Dealing with Stress

Here are some suggestions for dealing with stress:

- *Exercise*. When you are nervous, angry, or upset, release the pressure through exercise or physical activity. Run, jog, walk, Rollerblade, play tennis, work out in the gym, go for a swim, or do whatever you enjoy. Physical activity will help to relieve that uptight feeling.
- *Share* your stress. Find a friend, advisor, family member, or someone you can trust to talk to. You can also seek the help of a psychologist, psychiatrist, social worker, or mental health counselor if you feel that your problem is serious. If you need a place to turn, visit the health center at your college or university.
- *Know your limits*. If a problem is beyond your control and cannot be changed at the moment, don't fight the situation. Learn to accept what it is for now, until such time when you can change it.

○ *Take care of yourself.* Get enough rest and eat well. If you are irritable and tense from lack of sleep or if you are not eating correctly, you will have less ability to deal with stressful situations. Poor eating habits and lack of sleep are common problems that college students face. If you know you're not eating right, or if you're not getting enough sleep, take steps to remedy the situation immediately. Consult a doctor, if necessary. Having a restless night before taking exams can negatively impact your grades.

○ *Make time for fun.* There's more to college than test taking, attending classes, and studying. Sure, all these things are important, but college is also about having fun! Schedule time for both schoolwork and recreation. You need to make time to have fun and relax.

○ *Be a participant.* If you find that you're depressed, bored, or lonely, go to where it's all happening. Sitting alone can make you feel frustrated. Instead of feeling sorry for yourself, get involved in what's happening around you. If you want to know what's happening on your college campus, visit the student activities office or read the school's newspaper.

○ *Check off your tasks and get organized.* Trying to take care of everything at once can seem overwhelming, and as a result, you may not accomplish anything. Instead, make a list of what tasks you have to do, and then do them one at a time, checking them off as they're completed. Give priority to the most important tasks. Be sure to read the chapter called "Getting Organized" for additional tips on how to organize your life and relieve stress caused by having too many things to do and not having the time to do them.

○ *Avoid self-medication.* Although you can use prescription or over-the-counter medications to relieve stress temporarily, they do not remove the conditions that caused the stress in the first place. Medications can be habit forming and also can reduce your efficiency, thus creating more stress than they take away. The only time you should consider using any type of stress-relieving medication is when it's prescribed to you by a doctor.

One of the things that goes hand in hand with the college experience is stress. Those people who deal with stress the best are the ones who succeed. Since college is probably your first experience living alone (away from your family) as an adult, you'll be forced to make all sorts of decisions, deal with difficult people, manage your hectic schedule, and find time to party and have fun. It is important that you learn how to determine what causes the most stress for you, and then learn how to deal with that stress and relieve it. Letting stress build up inside can eventually cause problems that could have been avoided.

Some of the things that can cause stress while you're in college include:

- Disagreements with your roommate(s)
- Fights with your boyfriend/girlfriend
- Studying for upcoming exams
- Writing term papers
- Getting overwhelmed with too much homework
- Not getting along with a teacher or professor
- Getting sick, missing classes, and having to make up work
- Finding time for classes, studying, a job, and extracurricular activities
- Having a hangover the morning of an exam
- A surprise visit from your parents
- Running into financial problems
- Preparing for a major sporting event
- Having unprotected sex and worrying about the consequences (sexually transmitted disease, pregnancy, etc.)
- Lack of sleep or poor nutrition
- Dealing with an eating disorder, or drug, alcohol, or tobacco addiction (See help for this; don't try to deal with overcoming an addiction alone!)

○ *Avoid too much caffeine.* Drinking too much coffee, soda, or other caffeinated beverages can actually increase the stress you're experiencing. If you're having trouble sleeping or concentrating, or if you find that your hands are shaking after you drink a caffeinated beverage, it's time to cut back on the caffeine.

○ *Pinpoint what's causing your stress and change it.* If you can determine what's generating the stress in your life, then you should be able to discover ways to eliminate it.

○ *Take a hot shower or soak in a hot tub.* Tense muscles are a way your body has of telling you that it's under stress. If your shoulder or neck muscles are very tight due to stress, taking a hot shower can help you relax. There are also many simple physical and breathing exercises that you can do to help eliminate various types of physical and emotional stress. Self-hypnosis and yoga are also simple things you can do to help yourself relax. There are many books, videocassettes, and audio tapes at any library or bookstore designed to teach you basic breathing exercises and other stress-reducing activities.

Remember, stress builds up, especially if it's not dealt with. Once in a while, everyone has a stressful day when things just don't go well. However, if you find that you're under a lot of stress every day, then it's important that you take steps to deal with that stress. Don't be afraid to ask for help.

Dealing with Depression

Most people experience some form of depression at one time or another. In fact, during any six-month period, over nine million American adults suffer from a depressive illness. When young people experience depression, they often feel helpless, very alone, and beyond help. There's a big difference between getting depressed because you did poorly on a test or broke up with a boyfriend or girlfriend, and going through days, weeks, or months at a time feeling depressed. If you feel like you're in the latter category and you've been suffering for a long while and just can't seem to shake that feeling of helplessness or depression, then you need to seek professional help. You could be experiencing a depressive disorder that impacts your body, your mood, and your thoughts.

Depression can impact the way you eat and sleep, the way you feel about yourself, and how you think and react to the environment around you. This is *not* a personal sign of weakness, nor it is a condition that you're bringing upon yourself. If you're experiencing a depressive disorder and thinking about suicide or in any way harming yourself or someone else, then it's critical that you get yourself some help. You can get help and support that's free of charge and totally confidential by visiting the health center at your college, or by calling the local hospital in your city. Don't attempt to deal with strong feelings of depression on your own.

What Causes Serious Depression?

There are many causes of long-term depression, such as a serious loss, chronic illness, a difficult relationship, financial problems, or an unwelcome change in life patterns. Very often, a combination of genetic, psychological, and environmental factors is involved in the onset of a depressive disorder. The first step for curing this disorder is getting the appropriate treatment, starting with a physical and psychological examination by a doctor. Just about every form of depression can be helped and cured by medical professionals, but you have to take the first step and seek help by making an appointment with a medical doctor and describing your symptoms.

Signs of Depression

If you are experiencing several of the following symptoms of depression, please consider seeing a doctor or medical professional:

○ Loss of appetite and/or weight loss or overeating and weight gain
○ Decreased energy
○ Difficulty concentrating, remembering, and making decisions
○ A persistent sad, anxious, or "empty" mood
○ Fatigue
○ Feelings of guilt, worthlessness, and/or helplessness
○ Feelings of hopelessness and pessimism
○ Insomnia, early-morning awakening, or oversleeping
○ Loss of interest or pleasure in hobbies and activities that were once enjoyed, including sex

○ Persistent physical symptoms that do not respond to treatment, such as headaches, digestive disorders, and chronic pain
○ Restlessness and/or irritability
○ Thoughts of death or suicide; suicide attempts

It is important to realize that exhaustion, and feelings of helplessness, worthlessness, and hopelessness, are part of the depression and typically do not accurately reflect your situation. If you're experiencing depression, try to refrain from setting difficult goals for yourself or taking on lots of extra responsibilities. Try to be with other people. Participate in activities that make you feel better. When you're depressed, don't make any major life decisions, like whether to drop out of school. Don't get upset if your friends and people close to you don't understand what you're going through. The most important thing you can do if you're feeling very depressed and think you're experiencing some form of depressive disorder is to get the appropriate diagnosis and treatment, and then stick with the treatment that's prescribed by a professional.

WHERE TO FIND HELP IF YOU'RE DEPRESSED

The following are resources you can contact for help if you're experiencing depression. You don't have to deal with it alone!

○ See your family doctor or visit the medical center at your college/university.
○ Visit with a mental-health specialist, such as a psychiatrist or psychologist, a social worker, or mental-health counselor. (Your school most likely has a psychologist on staff that will help you, free of charge. Everything will be totally confidential.)
○ Visit a hospital's psychiatry department or outpatient clinic.
○ Check the yellow pages (of your phone book) under "Mental Health," "Health," "Social Services," "Suicide Prevention," "Hospitals," or "Physicians."

The Consumer Information Catalog also offers a free booklet called *Plain Talk* About... Depression, which you can obtain by writing to the Consumer Information Catalog, P.O. Box 100, Pueblo, Colorado, 81002. If you have access to the Internet, you can also download this publication from the Consumer Information Catalog's Web site (http://www.pueblo.gsa.gov).

Eating Disorders

Often, people with eating disorders won't admit it to themselves. After reading this section, if you believe that someone you know is suffering from an eating disorder, take it upon yourself to help them get help for themselves. You could save the life of your friend or loved one.

An eating disorder is NOT something you can deal with alone. Getting proper treatment for this type of disorder is critical—the sooner, the better. An eating disorder is a form of mental illness that can be treated successfully. If untreated, an eating disorder can become life threatening (in other words, it can kill you!). Young people, particularly young women, are the most vulnerable to eating disorders, which may result from going on strict diets in order to achieve an "ideal" figure. Chances are you've heard the terms *anorexia nervosa* and *bulimia nervosa*, the two most common forms of eating disorders.

We've all seen those television movies and episodes of *Beverly Hills 90210* that deal with eating disorders. Anorexia involves literally starving oneself to death; bulimia involves excessive overeating followed by vomiting or other purging behaviors to control weight.

Most people with eating disorders share certain personality traits: low self-esteem, feelings of helplessness, and a fear of becoming fat. In anorexia, bulimia, and binge eating, the disorder seems to develop as a way of handling stress and anxieties. People with anorexia tend to be "too good to be true." They rarely disobey, they keep their feelings to themselves, and they tend to be perfectionists. They are good students, and often excellent athletes. People who develop bulimia and binge eating disorders typically consume huge amounts of food—often junk food—to reduce stress and relieve anxiety. However, the binge eating is followed by

For additional information about eating disorders, call or write to any of the following groups or agencies:

National Association of Anorexia Nervosa and Associated Disorders (ANAD)
P.O. Box 7
Highland Park, IL 60035
(708) 831-3438

Anorexia Nervosa and Related Eating Disorders, Inc. (ANRED)
P.O. Box 5102
Eugene, OR 97405
(503) 344-1144

American Anorexia/Bulimia Association, Inc. (AABA)
418 East 76th Street
New York, NY 10021
(212) 734-1114

National Anorexia Aid Society (NAAS)
Harding Hospital
1925 E. Dublin Granville Road
Columbus, OH 43229
(614) 436-1112

Overeaters Anonymous
P.O. Box 92870
Los Angeles, CA 90009
(310) 618-8835

A free, 17-page booklet, called *Eating Disorders*, is available by writing to the Consumer Information Catalog, P.O. Box 100, Pueblo, Colorado, 81002. If you have access to the Internet, you can also download this publication from the Consumer Information Catalog's Web site (http://www.pueblo.gsa.gov).

guilt and depression. Purging can bring relief, but it is only temporary. The person with this disorder gets caught in a vicious cycle.

What's involved in the treatment of an eating disorder? It all depends how serious the situation has become. People who are on the verge of severe medical problems or death as a result of their condition need a comprehensive treatment plan, involving a variety of experts and approaches. Ideally, the treatment team will include an internist, a nutritionist, an individual psychotherapist, a group and family psychotherapist, and a psychopharmacologist—someone who is knowledgeable about psychoactive medications useful in treating these disorders. Sure, dealing with an eating disorder can be scary for the person experiencing it as well as for their friends and family, but the people who get help are the ones that get cured. For students, treatment programs may be available through a school's counseling or medical center.

CHAPTER

EMERGENCY ISSUES
WHERE TO GO FOR HELP... FAST

College is about having fun, learning, and having new experiences. Unfortunately, not all of your experiences will be joyous ones. Chances are, problems will arise. The best way to deal with any type of problem you experience while in school is to know where to turn for help. It's a great idea to keep a list of emergency phone numbers near your phone and in your wallet. This list should include phone numbers for:

○ Campus Security
○ Campus Health Center
○ Police
○ Fire Department
○ Ambulance/Paramedics
○ Personal Physician

Since you're not living at home anymore, make sure that your roommate or close friends are aware of any medical conditions or allergies you have, and any special treatment that you may require in case of emergency. Your roommate and/or close friends should also know how to contact your parents in case of emergency.

There's Always 911

If you get sick, injured, or have any type of medical emergency, your school offers a health center that should at the very least have a nurse on call twenty-four hours per day. When you register for school, you will get some type of health insurance. Make sure that you carry your health insurance card with you at all times. In case of a real emergency, you might consider going straight to a hospital emergency room or to an off-campus walk-in medical center.

Be sure to see a doctor or seek medical assistance if you get sick and have a fever that lasts for more than a day or two. If you experience an extremely high fever (over 101 degrees Fahrenheit), see a doctor immediately. Likewise, if you think you may have a broken bone, experience extreme dizziness or nausea, have problems urinating, have problems breathing, or experience symptoms that are unusual or severe for any extended length of time, see a doctor.

Most cities in America offer 911 emergency service. If necessary, you can always dial 0 and speak with an operator, who can refer you to an ambulance, hospital, or other emergency service.

Dental Care

Should you have problems with your teeth or gums (or any related dental issue) consult your school's health center about making an appointment with a dentist. If it's an emergency, check the Yellow Pages under "Dentists." Most dental practices will accept patients immediately if an emergency (such as a bad toothache) exists. Don't try to stop the pain of a toothache with medication and hope the problem goes away. Consult a dentist. At least twice per year, it's a good idea to schedule a routine checkup and cleaning with a dentist.

Eye Care

If you find yourself suffering from headaches, blurry vision, or other symptoms that relate to eye strain, then you should see an eye doctor immediately. In fact, you should make it a habit to see an eye-care professional once per year, especially if you currently wear any type of prescription eyeglasses or contact lenses.

It's always best to consult your family eye-care professional, if you have one. If not, there are eye-care professionals available to you at virtually every shopping mall (in those one-hour eyeglass stores) and stores like Wal-Mart. You can also consult the Yellow Pages or your school's medical center for a referral for an eye doctor located near your school.

If you need to order new eyeglasses or contact lenses, the least expensive places to go are Wal-Mart, Eye World, Pearl Vision Center, and Lenscrafters. Ask about special promotions that can save you money. For example, you may be able to get a free pair of prescription sunglasses (or a second pair of eyeglasses) with the purchase of one set of prescription lenses with frames. Make sure you ask your eye doctor for a copy of your prescription. Keep this prescription with you in your wallet, so if you ever lose your glasses or contacts, you can order a replacement quickly, no matter where you are.

Car Problems

If you have a car on campus, your best bet is to join an auto club, such as the American Automobile Association (AAA). These clubs offer a toll-free telephone number that you can call from anywhere, twenty-four hours per day, seven days per week, if you get stuck, run out of gas, get a flat tire, and so forth. For a few bucks extra, AAA offers AAA Plus, which features additional membership services, such as free towing for up to 100 miles. AAA also offers a complete travel agency service and can often save you money when planning trips.

To join AAA, call (800) AAA-HELP, or visit the AAA office in your city. Once you join an auto club, keep your membership card in your wallet.

Problems with a Faculty Member

If and when a problem arises with a faculty member, try approaching that professor privately, during his or her posted office hours, to discuss the situation. Assuming you can't reach a satisfactory solution with that professor, make an appointment to see the department head (chairperson), or contact your school's dean of students or vice president of student affairs. Your faculty advisor (if you have one) is the best person to turn to for assistance or referrals regarding whom to contact if a problem arises with a professor. Someone in the administration should be able to act as an arbitrator. Never wait until a situation gets out of hand.

Within the first few weeks of every semester, students are allowed to transfer or drop out of a class with no penalties. Should you decide that you don't like a faculty member or that a specific course isn't for you, transfer out of that class before the deadline.

Legal Problems

What happens if you get yourself arrested? Well, for starters, you should call your parents immediately! Yes, your parents are going to be really pissed off at you, but if you get arrested, you're in over your head, and this can have an impact on the rest of your life if you don't handle the situation correctly. Should you require the services of a lawyer, contact the Bar Association or Legal Aid office in your city and ask for a referral. If at all possible, use the services of a lawyer who knows you or your family

CHAPTER

DOING YOUR OWN LAUNDRY

SINCE UNDERWEAR ISN'T DISPOSABLE, WASH IT

O kay, you've made it to college. Are you ready for the many challenges that face you—like having to do your own laundry? Sorry, your mommy isn't around anymore to empty out your hamper once a week, do your laundry, iron your shirts, and then neatly fold your clothes, hang them up, or place them in your dresser drawers. That's your job now!

At first, the whole concept of doing your own laundry, without totally destroying your clothes, may seem a bit confusing. Have no fear . . . the folks at Procter & Gamble, the company that makes a zillion and one popular household products, like Tide laundry detergent, have developed easy-to-follow tips for doing laundry. Many of these laundry tips are included within this chapter, but if you have access to the Internet, be sure to visit the Tide ClothesLine Web Site (http://www.clothesline.com) for additional information.

The first rule of thumb for doing laundry while at college is to always save your quarters! Find yourself a big jar and place it on your dresser. Use this jar for storing your quarters. It'll typically cost you between $1.00 and $1.50 (in quarters) per load of wash; then you'll have to use the dryer, which costs an addi-

419 million loads of laundry are done each week by millions of people. You're about to become a statistic!

tional $1.00 to $1.50 (in quarters). Since the average person changes outfits (or at least underwear) at least once per day, by the end of each week, you'll have yourself a nice pile of laundry just waiting to be cleaned. Before starting to do your laundry, make sure you have enough quarters, or you could wind up with a load of wet clothes and not enough money to get them dry. It's also a good idea to have enough quarters for an extra wash or dry cycle, just in case a machine eats your money, or your clothes don't get totally dry.

Next, it's time to choose a laundry detergent. If you go to any supermarket, there are literally dozens of liquid and powder detergents to choose from. Laundry detergents come in many sizes, colors, and scents. If you want to save money, buy one large box or container of detergent so it will last you for several months. In terms of choosing the actual detergent you use, you can always call home and ask your mom what she recommends.

When it comes to choosing a detergent, the makers of Tide believe that some people want convenience, and others focus on cleaning power. Sometimes, people choose a detergent based on fragrance (or no fragrance). The type of water you have in your dorm (or where you do your laundry) can be a determining factor when selecting which detergent works best. For this reason, Procter and Gamble has developed an entire range of Tide products—which it refers to as the Tide Family of Products (you can write to the company if you want a family portrait for your dorm room).

Laundry detergents available as part of this Tide Family of Products include Tide Ultra 2 Powder, Tide Liquid (which can also be used to pretreat stains), Tide with Bleach, Tide with Bleach Alternative, and Tide Free (which contains no additives, dyes, or perfumes). Remember, these are just a few of the many detergents (from many manufacturers) that are available.

After you've collected your quarters, next, go on an expedition and locate the washing machine and dryer in your dorm or apartment complex (the basement is often a good place to begin your search). Once you've located the washer and dryer, READ THE DIRECTIONS ON THE MACHINE CAREFULLY BEFORE PROCEEDING!

Laundry Procedures

After you have your pile of laundry, your detergent (and optional stain remover and/or fabric softener), and your quarters, and have located the laundry room, it's time to actually do your laundry. Here are some useful prelaundering tips from Procter & Gamble:

1. Empty your pockets.
2. Turn down the cuffs on your pants and shirts.
3. Turn your jeans inside out (if you don't want them to fade as quickly).
4. Close all zippers, snaps, and hooks, and tie strings together.
5. Sort your clothes. Separate the dark colors, light colors, and whites. Also, sort your delicate fabrics from heavier ones, and keep lint-producing fabrics (such as terry robes and towels) separate. Also, set aside your very dirty clothes and wash them separately. All new clothes should be washed separately the first time (the dyes in your new clothes could spread to other clothes

and ruin them.) Large items, such as bedspreads, comforters, and king size blankets should be washed alone or laundered and dried in oversized machines, which are available at most laundromats.

6. Pretreat stains or heavily soiled areas of your clothes.

7. Read all labels carefully! Consider these little tags on your clothes to be your own personal laundry cheat sheets. Apparel care labels make sorting foolproof.

8. Since you're in college, you're probably smart enough to know that if a label on a garment says

WHAT YOU'LL NEED FOR YOUR LAUNDRY
- A laundry basket or laundry bag (to store your dirty clothes and transport them to the washing machine)
- Quarters
- Laundry detergent
- Fabric softener (optional)
- Stain remover (optional)

Dry Clean Only, you should NOT try to launder it yourself. Take it to a dry cleaner to get professionally cleaned.

Actually Doing Your Laundry

1. Choose the temperature and cycle settings on your washing machine. As a general rule, HOT = WHITES AND VERY DIRTY CLOTHES and COLD = DARK COLORS AND COLORS THAT RUN. Use WARM water for everything else. Yes, water temperature is important. It directly affects the performance of the laundry products used, the behavior of soil, the wrinkling of fabrics, and the durability of colors and fabric finishes.

If the label on your clothing or the directions on your laundry detergent say to use different temperatures, follow those temperature directions instead of these. Chances are, you'll be using a washing machine with automatic washer settings. The HOT setting draws water only from the hot water line and the temperature will be whatever the water heater in your dorm provides. Manufacturers design the normal or regular setting on most water heater thermostats to deliver in the range of 140 to 150 degrees Fahrenheit. The COLD water setting draws water only from the cold water line, so the temperature will be that of the water entering your dormitory laundry room. The WARM water setting provides essentially a 50/50 mixture of hot and cold water.

2. Empty all filters built into the washing machine.
3. Turn on the machine to fill it with water.
4. Add detergent only after the machine has begun to fill with water. Follow measuring ingredients on the package. The most common reason for unsatisfactory laundering results is not using the correct amount of detergent.
5. Add your dirty clothes to the washing machine. Be sure that you don't overload the washer by placing too many clothes into it.

CHOOSING THE RIGHT WATER TEMPERATURE

Water temperature directly affects cleaning and wrinkling. The proper choice of water temperature can also minimize dye transfer from unstable colors. Check your garment care labels for recommended wash temperature. If the care label advice isn't available, use the following as a guide:

o Hot water provides the quickest and best cleaning. Use it for sturdy whites, colorfast pastels and light prints, and heavily soiled work and play clothes.

o Warm water cleans while minimizing dye loss, removes wear wrinkles, and helps to reduce wrinkling in the washer. Use it for permanent press, all colorfast dark and bright colors, synthetics made of nylon, polyester, and acrylic, and washable woolens.

o Cold water may help protect sensitive dyes, minimize washer wrinkling, and save hot water. However, it doesn't clean as well as warmer temperatures. Use it for bright red and orange dyes that release color without losing intensity, lightly-soiled fabrics, and removal of some protein stains such as blood. COLD WATER IS EXCELLENT FOR RINSING ALL LOADS, REGARDLESS OF THE WASHING TEMPERATURE. Laundry detergents are formulated to clean well at temperatures above 60 degrees Fahrenheit.

Clothing needs room to circulate within the washer to obtain maximum cleaning.

6. To avoid excessive wrinkling, be prepared to remove your clothes as soon as the washing machine has completed its laundering process.

Remember, some fabrics and clothing products need special care. These garments should often be hand-washed to preserve them. Sweaters also require special care, since their fiber contents vary from cotton to wool. To prevent shrinkage, stretching, fading or bleeding, read the care tags on the garments and follow those directions carefully.

Dealing with Stains

According to the severity of soils/stains on your garments, the makers of Tide say that you may want to pretreat, presoak, or prewash:

○ Pretreat to remove a few small spots. Apply undiluted laundry detergent, such as Liquid Tide with Bleach Alternative; undiluted liquid dishwashing detergent, such as Dawn; or suds from an Ivory soap bar, directly on the stained area. Launder immediately.

○ Presoak for deep-set soils, old stains, extensive staining, or protein stains like blood, grass, or "body soils." Soak stained item(s) in a plastic bucket or laundry tub with the warmest water safe for the fabric and a

good heavy-duty laundry detergent, like Tide, for a maximum of thirty minutes. Bleach-sensitive stains, like fruit juice or drink mixes, should be rinsed in cold water, and then washed with a nonchlorine bleach product. If stains remain, colorfast items may be laundered with a colorfast bleach, like Biz®, and bleachable items may be laundered with chlorine bleach.

○ Prewash for heavily soiled garments, for example, work or play clothes. Run through the prewash cycle with the recommended amount of detergent. When the wash cycle is complete, drain the prewash solution and launder in the hottest water recommended by the manufacturer.

Drying Your Clothes

After the washing machine has done its thing, you'll find yourself with a heap of wet clothing on your hands. You could do like they did in the olden days and hang your clothes out to dry on a clothesline (but in a dormitory situation, that's probably not the best idea), or you could use a dryer.

Load your dryer so that the clothes can circulate. Overloading can result in excessive wrinkling. Heat damage to clothing can also result if the dryer

vent becomes blocked. Yet drying a load that's too small reduces the tumbling effect and prolongs the drying period. Tip: If you're going to be drying a small amount of clothes, add three or four already clean white towels to the dryer to speed up drying times. Once again, it's important to read the labels on your garments. Some fabrics, like 100 percent cotton, shrink in the dryer, unless the garment has been preshrunk by the manufacturer.

You may choose to add a fabric softener sheet, such as Bounce®, to help reduce static cling and to keep your clothes soft and smelling clean. Once again, read the directions on the fabric softener package before using.

Using proper drying procedures protects garments and minimizes wrinkling. Most dryers have delicate permanent press cycles, which have lower heat settings to protect fabrics that might be damaged by high heat. Check clothing care labels carefully for proper drying temperatures.

Remove clothing from the dryer as soon as the cycle ends. Hang or fold your clothes immediately to further reduce wrinkling.

A Few Other Laundry Tips

Since you will probably be doing your laundry in the dormitory and sharing the same machines with dozens of other students (or using a public laundromat), it's an excellent idea to stay with your clothes while they're in the washer and dryer. Otherwise, what you put in the machines might be missing: Clothes thieves are a reality in a dorm situation. Bring a book or study notes and get homework done while you're waiting for your clothes to get clean. If there are multiple washers and dryers in your laundry room, arrange to do your laundry at the same time as a friend, so you have someone to hang out with. If you can't sit and watch your clothes, determine exactly how long each washer and dryer cycle takes, and be there as soon as your clothes are done.

If you leave your clothes in a washer or dryer, someone who wants to use the machine may empty out your machine and could pile up your clothes on a nearby

table, on top of the machine, or on the dirty floor (so much for having clean clothes). When your clothes are lying around unattended, that's when they'll get stolen. Also, it's not a good idea to leave your empty laundry basket (or bag) and detergent sitting on or near the washer or dryer. People might choose to "borrow" them and you won't get them back.

To save waiting time (due to machines being in use), try to pick less busy times to do your laundry, such as weekday afternoons, early mornings, or very late nights. Weekends—particularly Sunday afternoons—and evenings are often the busiest times. It's an excellent idea to get into the habit of doing your laundry on a regular schedule, such as every Wednesday night. This will insure that you always have clean clothes to wear. You'll ultimately save time if you do small loads of laundry often, instead of waiting until everything you own needs to be cleaned, forcing you to run many loads.

Worse case scenario is that you bring home all your dirty laundry over school breaks, and have Mom show you one more time how to get it done.

EATING

CHAPTER

14

EATING
DORM DINING AND LATE-NIGHT MUNCHIES

ven if you're on the three-meals-per-day plan at your school, chances are you're going to get hungry and thirsty throughout the day or during a late-night study session. That's why it's important to have some "supplies" on hand.

For starters, you'll almost definitely want to buy or rent a portable refrigerator for your dorm room. This will allow you to store a small amount of perishable food (such as fruit), plus keep your juice, soda, and other drinks (whatever they may be) cold.

In addition to a refrigerator, a portable microwave oven will come in handy for making snacks and quick meals. With a microwave, you can quickly nuke up some microwave popcorn, heat up soup, boil water (for coffee, tea, or hot cocoa), or heat up a frozen dinner. Chef Boyardee, and several other companies, offer single-serving microwave meals, such as lasagna or spaghetti and meatballs. Despite what you might think, these actually taste pretty good if you're in a pinch for a decent hot meal.

Another useful cooking appliance is a Crock-Pot, which can be used to make soups, stews, and other nutritious and delicious meals very easily. Crock-Pots are cheap and very easy to use, but to cook something with them requires

access to fresh meats and vegetables, plus it's critical that you keep the Crock-Pot clean in between uses.

Finally, you'll want to purchase a good-sized airtight container in which you can store additional foods and munchies, like potato chips, pretzels, cookies, and so on. The reason for the sealable container is twofold. First, it'll help keep these foods fresh once you open their packaging, and second, storing your foods will keep bugs and other unwanted creatures away.

Most dorm buildings offer cooking facilities, so if you're planning on doing some serious cooking, that's where you'll want to do it. Avoid using a hot plate in your dorm room—they're dangerous, plus most schools don't allow them.

You'll always want to store a small amount of food in your room in case you get hungry. If, however, you find yourself "pigging out" in the middle of the night, or relying on chocolate bars to keep you going throughout the day, then you must change your eating habits. If your school is close to a supermarket or convenience store, instead of just keeping junk food on hand, bananas and other fruits and vegetables make great snacks that are much healthier.

Instead of buying glass or plastic plates and metal utensils (knives, forks, and spoons), it's a good idea to keep an assortment of paper plates and disposable plastic utensils on hand, so you can simply throw them out when you're done. This will eliminate the need to wash dishes, which most college students tend to avoid at all possible costs. The last thing you want lying around your dorm room is dirty dishes. They smell, they attract bugs, and they're messy, especially after they've been sitting for several days. Yes, in the long run, buying paper plates, disposable utensils, and paper cups is more expensive, but the convenience factor is important.

Keeping the environment in mind, avoid using plastic or wax-coated plates, and don't use Styrofoam cups for your hot beverages. Buy one or two mugs and wash them when you're done.

For coffee drinkers, keeping an inexpensive instant coffeemaker in your dorm is convenient, and if you get one with a timer, you can set it to have a hot cup of coffee ready for you when you wake up. Many manufacturers of instant coffee, like Folgers, now sell "coffee singles," which are tea-baglike packets of instant coffee that are individually wrapped and allow you to make one cup at a time. If keeping milk (for coffee or cereal) is difficult, try Parmalat Whole Milk. This type of milk comes in small, half-pint containers and requires no refrigeration until opened.

Wait until you actually get to school and settle in before purchasing a portable refrigerator, microwave oven, or other cooking gadgets. Discuss what you need with your roommate, based on the cooking facilities that are available in your dorm building and your personal needs.

Try to Maintain a Healthy and Well-Balanced Diet

All foods contain combinations of nutrients and other healthful substances; but no single food can supply all of the nutrients in the amount you need to stay healthy. In other words, don't keep eating the same meal(s) every day. A well-balanced diet means eating the recommended number of daily servings from each of the five major food groups. Foods from the grain products group, along with vegetables and fruits, are the basis for a healthy diet. Meals that include rice, pasta, potatoes, or bread and that are accompanied by other vegetables and fruit, along with lean and low-fat foods from the other groups, are ideal.

Enjoy eating as wide a variety of foods as possible. Get the many nutrients your body needs by choosing among the various food groups, which include grain products, vegetables, fruits, milk and milk products (dairy), protein-rich plant foods (beans, nuts, etc.), and protein-rich animal foods (lean meat,

poultry, fish, and eggs). Whenever possible, choose low-fat foods. Keep in mind that some foods like stews and soups contain servings from multiple food groups (they often contain meat, beans, noodles, and vegetables). Thus, eating a well-balanced and healthy diet can be a lot easier than you might think.

As a college student, you're not always going to be eating healthy meals. In fact, you'll probably find yourself ordering a lot of pizza or Chinese food to be delivered to your dorm room (for example, on nights when you have to cram for a test or finish a term paper). If you know you're going to be eating a less than healthy dinner, make it a point to have something that's healthy for lunch. Sorry, a candy bar and a soda don't count. Instead of stocking junk food in your dorm, try to keep a stash of fresh fruits and vegetables, like carrot sticks, apples, and oranges. Even peanut butter and jelly sandwiches are healthier than a meal from a fast-food restaurant.

To learn more about nutrition and your health, consult a doctor, or read the pamphlet *Nutrition and Your Health: Dietary Guidelines for America* (file-name: dietary.txt), which is available, free of charge, on the Internet at http://www.pueblo.gsa.gov.

Taking vitamin and mineral supplements, such as One-A-Day or Centrum, will help you to meet your nutritional needs; however, these supplements do not supply all of the nutrients and other substances that healthy foods contain. If you believe your diet isn't healthy, consult a doctor or medical expert before taking any type of vitamin or mineral supplements. If you do take these nonprescription supplements, follow the directions on the packaging. Taking too many supplements, or taking certain supplements on an empty stomach, can actually be harmful to your health.

A Few Words About Alcohol

If you're under the legal drinking age, it's illegal to purchase, consume, or store alcoholic beverages. But chances are, you already knew that. Drinking beer in college, especially at parties, has unfortunately become almost as commonplace as drinking a soda.

If you don't drink, don't feel that you have to start just because you're about to begin college. One easy way to say no when you're out with a group of friends is to volunteer to be the designated driver, or the one responsible for getting everyone in the group back to the dorm safely. If these people are your friends, they'll understand that you don't drink and they'll accept that without giving you too much of a hassle.

How to Recognize a Drinking Problem

As a college student, you are the target audience for a multimillion-dollar per year advertising campaign that's designed to make alcohol seem appealing. The alcohol and beer companies use all forms of advertising to convince you that drinking alcohol is socially acceptable and enjoyable. All sorts of flashy and exciting ads are created to appeal directly to people in the eighteen to thirty-four age group. Advertising agencies make a fortune creating new and exciting ways to get people, like you, to taste test various types of beer and alcoholic beverages. If you believe these ads, having a few beers at a party isn't just acceptable, it's expected. If you want to capture the attention of that gorgeous guy or girl at a party, you have to have a beer in your hand. Guess what? This is advertising—not real life!

Many people start out believing the ads they see on TV, hear on the radio, or read in magazines, then they give in to peer pressure and start drinking. If you think you might have a drinking problem, or if there's someone you know who you think drinks too much, start by asking yourself these questions:

○ Do you, or someone you know, crave alcohol?

○ When you attend a party do you have to get totally drunk?

○ Do you drink on weeknights, or need to have a drink or two before going to class?

○ Do you often drink alone in your dorm or at a bar in order to forget your problems or to relieve stress?

○ Do you drive your car while under the influence of alcohol?

○ In a social situation, do you often have more than one or two drinks?

○ Do you find yourself blacking out and/or not remembering events as a result of your drinking?

○ Have family members or friends made comments about how much alcohol you consume, or have they suggested you have a drinking problem, but you deny it?

○ Do you have problems performing sexually after drinking?

○ Starting today, could you go for one month without consuming any alcohol (including beer)?

If you answered "yes" to any of these questions, then you or the person you know could have a drinking problem or an addiction to alcohol. Having an addiction to alcohol, drugs, or tobacco isn't something to be ashamed of, and it isn't something that you should deal with alone. Your family and friends don't have to know about your problem; however, breaking your addiction will be easier if you have the love and support of the people who are close to you.

If you know someone who you think has a drinking problem, chances are you're in a difficult situation. You can confront that person, but chances are, they'll deny having a problem. What do you do then? If you have a friend, roommate, or relative who you believe drinks too much, speak with someone confidentially at your school or call Alcoholics Anonymous

at (800) 835-1935. You don't have to give out a name in order to learn what you can do to help someone with a drinking problem.

Just about everyone has heard stories about college girls who were partying with guys (either at your school or at another school). Everyone had too much to drink, and one young woman ended up being raped or date raped. If you're a female, be smart. Don't hang out and party alone with one or more guys who are too drunk to know what's happening around them. Never party alone with strangers. You don't want things to get out of hand. Likewise, don't put yourself in a position in which you're at a party (or even drinking with male friends) and you're too drunk to know what's going on around you. There is no excuse for a guy having sexual relations with a woman if it isn't totally consensual. However, women can protect themselves by not getting into a situation where things get out of control as a result of too much alcohol. Whether you're a guy or girl, if you're going to drink, be responsible!

PART THREE:

THE SOCIAL SCENE

CHAPTER

15

ROOMMATES
GETTING TO KNOW THEM AND SHARING SPACE

You're about to move into a dorm room that could very well be smaller than a prison cell, and at the same time, you'll be forced to live with one or more total strangers. Don't worry, it's almost never as bad as it sounds. In fact, you could be about to meet your new best friend.

For some people, college roommates become lifelong friends; for others, a roommate becomes the biggest problem they face while in school. The third possibility, and perhaps the most common, is that you will develop a casual friendship with your new roommate(s). You'll get along well enough so as not to kill each other, but each of you will lead your own lives, and have your own circle of friends.

If you want your experience with your new roommate(s) to be positive, the trick is to establish an open line of communication. Set ground rules immediately. Upon getting accepted into a school, the housing department probably sent you a questionnaire if you chose to live in on-campus housing. This questionnaire asked personal questions about your living habits. Your answers are used to match you to a compatible roommate (or roommates). Thus, it is important that you answered the questions in this questionnaire honestly.

As soon as you find out who your roommate is going to be, call that person and introduce yourself. Try to find out as much as you can about him or her. If, for example, you are a nonsmoker and the school has matched you up with someone who smokes and that bothers you, request to have your roommate switched immediately. During your initial discussions with your new roommate, coordinate what you will be bringing with you to school. For example, you only need one television, stereo, telephone, and answering machine.

Some of the issues you'll have to work out with your roommate early on are:

- Find out specific times during the day or evening when you'll be able to quietly study in your room.
- Since you'll probably be sharing a telephone, work out a system for taking messages and dividing the phone bill.
- Talk about how you each plan to respect each other's privacy by setting boundaries and limits. A small space shared with other people doesn't afford much privacy.
- If you have a private bathroom, kitchen, or dining area, divide the chores involved in keeping those areas clean. If one of you is a total slob, work out an agreement

where you'll each keep your stuff (dirty clothes, etc.) on your own side of the room, or in your area. One roommate should not have to clean up after another, or live in another person's mess.

○ Set rules about overnight guests of the same or opposite sex. Adding another person to your already-crowded dorm room, even for a night or two, is an inconvenience to everyone. Consider limiting overnight guests to Friday and/or Saturday nights only.

○ When you're trying to sleep, you don't want your roommate sitting a few feet from you and talking on the phone all night with a boyfriend or girlfriend, or listening to a stereo or television without headphones. Talk about ways to solve these problems before they happen.

○ Set aside personal space for everyone in the room. For example, set a rule that under no circumstances is a roommate allowed to open and rummage through another person's dresser drawers or closet, or search under another person's bed. Everyone has to respect other

people's stuff, and should not "borrow" anything without permission. As new types of potential conflicts come up, spend a few minutes to work them out.

○ Respect other people's privacy. If you're about to enter into your dorm room and you notice the door its locked, take a moment to knock before entering. If each room in your dormitory has its own bathroom, determine how you're going to share it without infringing on the other person's privacy. If you both have an early morning class, decide beforehand who will wake up and take their shower first. This will avoid arguments or situations where you are late for class.

Demonstrating common courtesy will go a long way toward everyone getting along. If you've never had a roommate before, just having another person around is going to take some getting used to. After all, you're going to be getting dressed and undressed in front of this person on a daily basis, and you're going to be spending a lot of time with each other. Everyone at first feels a bit modest in front of strangers. This is totally normal. Everyone has to get used to sharing a room and a bathroom with others.

If there's something about how your roommate acts that makes you uncomfortable, discuss it with him or her. Everyone has what someone else might consider to be strange or unusual habits, so be prepared to compromise. Since you're going to be learning some very personal stuff about your roommate (and vice versa), agree to keep certain things just between yourselves, and trust will eventually develop.

Assuming your roommate is a total stranger and you're both incoming freshmen, chances are you both know very few people on campus. At least for the first few days or weeks of school, until you and your roommate(s) start meeting lots of people, try spending time together. Go to lunch or dinner together, and participate in activities together. Whatever you do, don't just sit in your room and watch TV. It's important that you get involved with the social scene on campus during those first few weeks, and having someone, like your new roommate, to do things

with will make everything a bit less stressful.

The easiest and best way to get to know your roommate is to spend time with him or her, and to be open and honest about yourself during your conversations. Find interests that you have in common, and use those common interests as a basis for becoming friends. This will take time, so don't worry about rushing it. If you begin having serious problems with your roommate, and you can't seem to work them out by finding common ground, seek outside help from the school— before things get out of hand! You can start by talking to the resident advisor (RA) in your dorm, or contacting your school housing office.

Moving into a dorm and living with one or more roommates is one of the best chances you're going to get in life to make new friends. Take advantage of this opportunity. If you were planning to share a dorm room with a high school pal, you might consider splitting up and living in the same dorm, but in different rooms. This way, you can stay

friendly, but you also have the opportunity to meet new people. If you're always hanging around with a friend from high school, it is very difficult for someone new to get to know you.

GET A
SOCIAL LIFE

CHAPTER

16

GET A SOCIAL LIFE

MEETING NEW FRIENDS

You're in a new environment that's filled with people, just like you, who are new to the area, don't know other people, and are close to your age. Yup, it's a perfect opportunity to start meeting new people and making new friends. But where should you start?

While your roommate(s) may not turn out to be your new best friend(s), spending time together as you begin exploring your new surroundings is a great place to start. It's a lot easier to meet new people, and visit new places, when you do it with other people. The trick is to meet as many people as you possibly can as early in your first semester as possible. The easiest way to do this is to actively participate in the freshmen orientation program that your school offers. Even if you're totally shy, just showing up for these events and participating in them will help you to meet people. Everyone who attends the orientation is looking to meet other people, and everyone is just as nervous as you are.

As you meet new people, and you find some that share the same interests as you, make plans. The best way to get to know people is to strike up a conversation with them. Start by making conversation about easy topics. Strike up a conversation with someone by asking:

○ Where are you from?
○ How did you wind up at this school? What made you choose it?
○ What are you going to be studying? What do you think your major will be?
○ What dorm are you living in?

You can also talk about current movies, how the school's various sports teams are expected to perform this year, or where you both like to shop for clothes. There's an age-old piece of wisdom that says avoid talking about religion or politics when you're in the company of strangers or new acquaintances. These topics usually lead to disagreement, and arguing with someone isn't the best way to strike up a friendship.

After orientation, classes will begin. Once again, here's an opportunity to meet people. Show up for your classes a few minutes early, and make a point to introduce yourself to the people you're sitting near. Before class is an excellent time to strike up a quick conversation. During your conversations, explore the possibility of setting up a study group.

One of the great things about colleges and universities is that they offer a tremendous variety of extracurricular activities you can easily get involved in.

Here's a guaranteed way of meeting people that share the same interests as you. Check with the student activities office at your school and pick up a directory of student organizations. Also, start reading the school newspaper to discover what's happening on campus.

Whether you're into sports, politics, religion, journalism, music, animals, community service, or drama, chances are your school offers many opportunities for you to become involved with student organizations that cater to your interests. If you're living off campus (either in an apartment or at home), these student activities are even more important, because they'll be one of your links to the campus.

Here's just a sampling of the types of organizations you might consider joining:

- A sorority or fraternity
- An on-campus religious organization (Hillel, Orthodox Christian Fellowship, etc.)
- The choir, glee club, band, or orchestra
- The drama, ballet, or dance clubs
- The gay and lesbian association
- A sport or athletic activity (skiing, rugby, golf, tennis, volleyball, soccer, football, basketball, rowing, squash, swimming, lacrosse, hockey, track and field, horseback riding, snow boarding, sailing, paintball, cycling, hiking, wrestling, fencing, etc.)
- Your school newspaper, TV, or radio station
- Volunteer organizations
- Student government
- An international organization
- The ROTC
- An organization based around your academic interests (e.g., astronomy, math, or computer clubs)

Early in the semester, the RA (resident advisor) or RD (resident director) of your dorm will most likely hold a dorm meeting. Here's another awesome opportunity to meet the people who you'll be living with. During this meeting, the RA or RD will set some ground rules for living in the dorm and talk about when the "quiet hours" are and what the policy is on alcohol consumption. There also might be opportunities to sign up for intramural sports or other dormwide activities. Even if attendance is not mandatory, make a point of attending these dorm meetings.

Meeting new people outside of your classes and your dorm building might take a bit of creativity, but there are plenty of things you can do to meet new friends. Walking up to a total stranger and striking up a conversation isn't always easy, especially for someone who is shy, but it gets easier with practice. Start off by attending organized events and activities, such as freshmen orientation, that are designed to help new students meet each other. If you know upperclassmen, hang out with them for a few days or evenings and have them introduce you to their friends. Make an

effort to join groups or organizations that interest you. You'll find that it's much easier to strike up a conversation with someone who has common interests.

As a general rule, when you meet someone new, try to establish common interests early in the conversation. For example, do you both have the same professors? Do you like the same types of movies? Are you both fans of the same sports team? Do you have the same major? The earlier in your freshmen year that you begin pursuing new friendships and acquaintances, the better off you'll be. If you have a roommate or a friend you enjoy hanging out with, bring them along to activities and work together to meet new people.

Here are a few additional suggestions for things you can do to meet new people:

○ Participate in organized student activities. Check the bulletin boards around campus, along with the college newspaper, for information about on-campus activities, such as organized parties, discussion groups, and off-campus trips.
○ Join an on-campus religious organization. Most schools have student-run religious organizations that sponsor organized

group activities and provide a place for you to meet new people with similar religious backgrounds and interests.

○ Join a fraternity or sorority. Upon joining a fraternity or sorority, you will instantly have a new group of "best friends." There are many pros and cons to joining a Greek organization, so find out what each group offers, and meet the current members before pledging.

○ Participate in intramural sports. You might not be an all-star athlete, but if you love participating in team sports, intramural sports is a fun and easy way to get involved, meet people, and get exercise.

○ During peak hours, go to the athletic center at your school and work out on the various exercise machines.

○ Eat meals in on-campus dining rooms. When it comes to eating meals, go to the on-campus dining room during the most busy times and make it a point to sit at a crowded table. Try to strike up conversations with the people eating around you.

○ Get a part-time job. If meeting new friends is important to you, try to land a job that requires you to work with people. For example, try getting a job at your school's bookstore or at a local off-campus hangout.

○ Hang out at the student union, the library, or any place that students gather to study or socialize. Don't be afraid to walk up to someone who is sitting alone and introduce yourself. You can strike up a conversation simply by asking for change for the soda machine.

○ Attend group study sessions. Every major academic department on campus should have some type of organized study hall or extra-help center that is open to all students. If you're having trouble in a course, drop by one of these study centers and you'll find groups of students having similar difficulties. Find a few people and form a study group. If you don't know where to find these groups, ask your professors. If you excel in a specific subject, you might want to volunteer in one of these centers and offer help to fellow students.

○ When you're spending time in your dorm room, keep the door open so people walking by can drop in to say hello.

Nonsocial Activities to Avoid

There are several activities that will entertain you, but are guaranteed to keep you from meeting new people. If you want to meet new friends, avoid these activities:

○ Avoid going to a movie alone. If you want to see a movie, ask a few people to join you.

○ Avoid studying in your dorm. You have to study; so do it in a place, such as a library, where you'll have the opportunity to interact with new people. Unless you're studying for an important exam, need time alone to do serious studying, or require total quiet to concentrate, don't sit alone in your dorm room.

○ Avoid watching TV alone in your dorm. Sitting alone watching Beverly Hills 90210, Melrose Place, Home Improvement, Star Trek: Voyager, Monday Night Football, or Wheel of

Fortune is a way of passing time, but it won't help you make new friends. If you have time to watch TV while you're in college, invite a few people over, make popcorn, and have a miniparty. Forget about being a couch potato. Do something interactive and social.

CHAPTER 17

Joining a fraternity or sorority is about making new friends and experiencing new things. Jason Pierce is the Director of Communications and Alumni Relations of Lambda Chi Alpha, Inc., one of the largest men's general fraternities with 255 chapters throughout North America. In this interview, Jason discusses what fraternities (and sororities) are all about.

"When I was a freshman at Elon College in North Carolina, I was interested in joining a fraternity, but couldn't find one at the time that I was interested in. Instead, I found a group of people that were interested in starting a chapter of a national fraternity on our campus, and we chose to affiliate ourselves with Lambda Chi Alpha," recalls Jason.

According to Jason, "Every fraternity and sorority is based on a different set of values or offers a different focus on values. There are many stereotypes and misconceptions about fraternities and sororities. What a lot of people don't truly understand is what these organizations are all about—which is a sense of belonging. These are organizations that are in existence for its members and provide services to members that enhance their undergraduate collegiate experience. They offer an outlet for students to get involved and meet lots of people. They provide the strong support of friendship from fellow students and alumni. It's a family away from home."

Who joins fraternities and sororities? Jason says that joining this type of organization is a two-way street. "The individual must actively want to become friends and become part of the organization, and at the same time, the organization must want that individual to become a member. The best time to begin thinking about joining a fraternity or sorority is in your senior year of high school, or when you begin college. Many colleges and universities now allow recruitment as soon as someone graduates from high school, so during the summer before their freshmen year in college is when potential members can make contact with fraternities or sororities at the college they'll be attending. A lot of Greek organizations offer on-campus housing, which is another benefit of membership. When you move into a fraternity house, you'll be living with your closest friends. You're in the company of the people you have chosen to spend your time with. Living in a fraternity house is very different from living in a typical dormitory or residence hall."

Fraternities and sororities are always changing in an effort to cater to their members and provide the benefits and services that members want. One thing that remains constant, however, is the dedication toward developing personal character and value among all members, in an effort to create leaders of the future.

If you're interested in joining a fraternity or sorority, Jason recommends that you contact your college's Greek office or the student affairs office to find out what Greek organizations are represented on your campus. Find out when the formal recruitment period for the Greek organizations takes place, and then make contact with members of the fraternities or sororities you're interested in joining. "Don't join an organization just because of its national reputation. Join a fraternity or sorority because you really like the people who are members of the chapter you'll be joining. Find the people you feel comfortable with and join that organization. These are going to be your friends for the rest of your life, so when you're applying for membership, don't put up a front or a false image. Be yourself! You want to find people who have similar interests and goals as you do," says Jason. "I would recommend that as an incoming college freshman, don't choose a fraternity or sorority based on your first introduction. Look at multiple fraternities or sororities that are on your campus before making a decision."

Despite everything that you've heard about what's involved with joining a fraternity or sorority, on almost every college/university campus in America, hazing is illegal. No longer does joining one of these Greek organizations mean that you'll be humiliated, spanked with a paddle, or forced to drink until you pass out. If you are asked (or forced) to participate in any type of hazing ritual that you're uncomfortable with, walk away!

Finally, a word about legacies: If one of your parents was involved in a Greek organization when they were in college, chances are you'll be invited to join that fraternity or sorority. Remember, the organization your parent joined a generation ago has undergone many changes over the years, so do your homework and meet the people presently involved with the organization to determine if you want to join.

Using your computer, you can find out about specific fraternities and sororities, and discover what Greek organizations are active on your college campus. Visit the Greek Pages World Wide Web site (http://www.greekpages.com).

As you attempt to learn about the Greek organizations that are active on your campus, here are some questions you can ask current members to help you determine if the specific fraternity or sorority is right for you:

○ What sets the fraternity or sorority you're interested in apart from others?

○ What type of time requirement is required of members?

○ What's involved in the pledging process?

○ What are the annual dues (membership fees)?

○ What type of community service or charity work does the organization participate in?

○ Can freshmen obtain leadership positions within the organization?

○ Does the organization maintain a test file (a collection of old exams) that members can use for studying?

○ Does the organization participate in intramural sports?

○ Is the organization active on campus?

○ Does the organization honor legacies?

○ What academic support is provided by the organization?

○ How much interaction and support does the organization get from alumni?

○ Does the Greek organization have a religious affiliation? (Almost every religion has at least one well-established, national Greek organization that is open only to members of a specific religion.)

Fraternities and sororities have their own lingo, which you should understand before you begin pledging:

○ An *active* member is someone who has been initiated as a lifelong member of a Greek organization.

○ An *alumna* or *alumnus* is a member of a Greek organization who has graduated from college.

○ An *associate member* refers to someone who has accepted a bid for membership, and is preparing for initiation, but has not yet been initiated as a full member.

○ A *bid* is an invitation to join a Greek organization.

○ Once someone has achieved full membership in a fraternity, they are referred to by other members as a *brother.* Likewise, a member of a sorority is referred to as a *sister* by other members.

○ *Dry rush* refers to an alcohol-free rush function or activity.

○ *Greeks* are members of a fraternity or sorority.

○ *Hazing* is any conduct that subjects a person to anything that might endanger, abuse, degrade, or intimidate them as a condition for membership in a Greek organization. Hazing is officially outlawed on college campuses.

○ A *house* is the residence where members of a Greek organization live. A *house* can also be a reference to a Greek organization.

○ The *interfraternity council (IFC)* is a governing body of campus fraternities that is made up of members from each Greek organization on campus.

○ To becoming a member of a Greek organization, a pledge must experience an *initiation* ceremony.

○ A *pledge* refers to someone who is actively trying to become a member of a Greek organization—someone who has been accepted as a member but is not yet a full member.

○ *Rush* is the process or period of time in which Greek organizations recruit new members. Thus, a *rushee* is someone who hopes to join a Greek organization and participates in that organization's rush activities.

Is Greek Life Really For You?

Fraternities and sororities are definitely group-oriented organizations that appeal to people who are very social. People in these Greek organizations tend to be part of close-knit groups that live, eat, and socialize together. Thus, the members tend to have similar interests, and little privacy. If you don't consider yourself to be very social, or you don't enjoy spending all of your time with the same group of people, even if they are your friends, then Greek life is probably not for you. Greek life is a very different way of life than simply living in a dorm room and attending classes. Most Greek organizations have a well-defined behavior code that you must agree to live by. Joining a Greek organization also means taking on countless social responsibilities that will be above and beyond your academic, extracurricular, and job responsibilities. When a fraternity or sorority holds any type of activity, members of that organization are expected to attend. Think about the time, emotional commitment, and financial commitment that's required, and talk to members of the Greek organization you're interested in joining before pledging.

CHAPTER

COLLEGE SPORTS

FOR SUPERSTAR ATHLETES AND WEEKEND (OR AFTER CLASS) WARRIORS

At many schools the sports program is something that rallies together much of the student body—some as athletes and the rest as spectators. Intramural sports offer just about every student, regardless of their athletic ability, an opportunity to participate in their favorite sport, simply by signing up. Many schools offer extensive intramural programs that encompass many different individual and team sports. Students who participate in intramural sports programs have the opportunity to play their favorite sport, get exercise, and meet new friends.

For those who are more talented and dedicated, participating in NCAA sports becomes much more serious, and requires far greater time and emotional commitment. Norb Garritt is the editor of *College Sports* magazine. He has a lot of advice to offer to potential college athletes.

"Your opportunity for becoming a member of a college team is often based on the achievements you establish while in high school. The tough part for any athlete about to begin college is getting noticed. A lot of parents have taken on the job of serving as a public relations person for their son or daughter when it comes to marketing them to potential colleges.

Many high school coaches are well aware of how to best place their athletes who are looking to attend college, but some high school coaches just don't care, which means it's up to the student and their families to capture the attention of college recruiters. If you know you want to play soccer in college, for example, you're going to know by your sophomore or junior year of high school if you're good enough to play at the college level. That generally means being in the top third of your high school team from a talent standpoint," explains Norb.

"To participate in sports at some upper-echelon universities, you absolutely, positively, must have good grades plus superior athletic abilities to get admitted both into the school and onto a team. The top schools can choose from the cream-of-the-crop in terms of incoming freshmen. As long as you meet the minimum NCAA requirements in terms of your grades, you can still go to an excellent athletic university, because you're eligible for any Division I school out there," adds Norb.

Becoming a college athlete often means making a year-round commitment to your team, because you're expected to spend the off-season in the weight room and in training. The expectations on you as a college athlete are that you'll be working on your game year-round. "You need to be prepared to balance a full athletic load, and also manage a full academic schedule. It's a lot of pressure, and a lot of people can't take it, especially if they're not totally prepared. It's not easy by any stretch of the imagination, but as long as you understand the expectations and the

One thing to look out for is agents. Don't get involved with anyone who offers you something that's too good to be true, or something that doesn't seem 100 percent ethical. Don't accept any type of gift, whether it's a T-shirt or a free trip. Don't do anything that could sacrifice your athletic career, your academic career, or your future. Should you have any questions, speak with your high school coach or contact the NCAA directly. A legitimate agent can help you, but some people are out simply to make a buck at your expense.

pressures you'll face, you can handle it," explains Norb. "The biggest mistake college athletes make is taking their academics for granted. You have to understand that the coaches at the college level are there to help you get better personally, academically, and athletically, but their job is also to insure that their team's ledger has more wins than losses. Often, athletes tend to go to college with a jaded concept that the school is there to help them all the time, and that's not the case. It's up to you, the athlete, to go in knowing what it is you want to accomplish. If you don't recognize that getting your degree is as important, if not more important, than scoring, then that's a major mistake."

According to Norb, star high school athletes that get recruited by colleges or universities should be looking for several things when exploring their options:

○ Is the school that's trying to recruit you offering you an opportunity to contribute quickly? You want to go in and play. It's not easy to go from star status in high school to riding the bench at the college level. If you're going to a school that has six top-ranked sophomores in the year that you're going to be entering as a freshman, then the chances of you actually becoming an active member of your school's team are slim.

○ Take a look at the coach and the administration. Does the school have a good track record? Ask to see the graduation rates of the athletes over the past five years. You also want to see the transfer rates of the athletes, to determine what percentage wind up leaving the school before earning their degree.

○ Does the school offer courses that cater to your academic interests? If you're a star athlete, but you also have a strong interest in computers, for example, then you want to attend a school that has a strong computer science department. A lot of college athletes wind up transferring schools, not because they didn't like their coach, but because they realized that the school didn't support their academic interests with the appropriate types of classes. As an incoming freshman, it's important to have at least a general idea of what you want to major in, or what type of career you might be interested in pursuing outside of athletics.

One final piece of advice Norb has for college athletes is to pursue all scholarship opportunities that are available. "A lot of times parents ignore the athletic scholarship opportunities that are available, because they don't believe that their family fits the necessary income criteria. There are so many scholarship opportunities out there, especially for the less popular sports, like tennis and golf, and many college athletes don't go after them. If you have any athletic talent at all, you should look into what scholarship opportunities are available. Call a few colleges and universities and ask what types of scholarships are available for someone with talent in the sport you're interested in."

To subscribe to *College Sports* magazine so that you can stay up to date on all that's happening in all aspects of college sports, call (800) 722-2346. The magazine has over a million readers and offers in-depth features on players, coaches, and teams; special reports that tackle key issues; pro draft previews for all major sports; recruiting news; and preseason previews in all popular college sports.

A Few Words from Jim O'Brien, Men's Basketball Coach, Boston College

For college athletes participating in an intercollegiate sport, their coach often has a bigger impact on their lives than their friends, professors, and even their parents. Jim O'Brien is the Head Coach for the Men's Basketball Team at Boston College. In the following interview, he offers some useful advice to anyone interested in becoming a college athlete.

Q: What type of commitment do college athletes have to make to their team?

A: It really depends on what level the athlete will be playing at. If athletes are going to participate in Division-III-level sports, they won't be getting financial aid or scholarships based on their athletic abilities. When those kids participate in a sport, there's not the same level of commitment required, because they don't owe anything to the school. For someone who gets recruited into a Division-II- or a Division-I-level sport, the athlete has to make a very big commitment. For example, with our basketball program, kids return to school on September 5th, and after one week at school, they begin a one-month intensive conditioning program that includes running, weight lifting, and basketball practice for several hours per day. This is in addition to their full academic schedule. After the conditioning program is over, team members must practice six days per week, for an average of two hours per day.

Q: What advice can you offer for juggling a full academic schedule with a team schedule?

A: Develop a structure and a schedule. The biggest problem that college freshmen have is the inability to budget their time. In high school, your time is pretty well budgeted for you. In college, your day is a lot less structured, yet you have responsibilities that you're required to fit into your daily schedule. People need to learn how to manage their time and use their free time in a productive way.

Q: Should college athletes rely on their coaches to help them manage their academic requirements as well as their athletic schedules?

A: It's ultimately the student's job to insure that academic requirements are being met; however, many schools offer academic advisors for college athletes. At Boston College, we have a program on our campus, called Learning Resources for Student Athletes. Its function is to oversee the academic progress of the athletes, ranging from making sure that they're taking the appropriate courses that will allow them to make normal progress toward earning their degree while simultaneously juggling their schedule to coincide with our practice times. It also coordinates tutorial help in all subjects, and monitors each ath-

lete's class participation. All of the coaches at Boston College also randomly check each student's class attendance, so we know how much class time our student athletes are missing. A school can only do

so much. The students themselves have to be motivated to get their schoolwork accomplished on their own. There's an old saying: You can lead a horse to water, but you can't make him drink. In our case, we can offer students all types of services and tutors, but we can't make them do their school work and earn good grades.

Q: When conflicts between courses and athletics come up, which should take priority?

A: Academics always take priority. We try to do the best job possible to insure that classes never conflict with our practice schedules. Obviously, this can't be done 100 percent of the time, so special accommodations sometimes are made. If a class meets during a practice, the athlete is expected to attend class, and work something out with the coach.

Q: What are the biggest misconceptions that most incoming college freshmen have about college sports?

A: Probably, the biggest misconception is that in college, you're not going to have to do any work if you're a gifted athlete, and that's not the case. Our athletes at Boston College have to take the same courses as everyone else, and they have to achieve a certain grade-point average to remain eligible to participate in the school's sports program. People think that schools will slide their best athletes through, just to keep them eligible, but that is not at all accurate.

Q: What's the biggest mistakes you've seen college athletes make?

A: Not spending enough time on their schoolwork, and not managing their free time correctly.

Q: Is there anything else that you think potential college athletes should know?

A: Coming out of high school, a lot of athletes must decide if they're going to attend their first-choice school, where they may or may not have a chance play the sport that interests them, or if they're going to attend a school that might be fifth or sixth on their list of choices, but that guarantees them a chance to participate in an intercollegiate sport. Many students sacrifice the opportunity to attend a school they want to go to for an opportunity to play on a team. My advice for the 95 percent or more who will never get an opportunity to play professionally is that they should focus on going to a school that they want to attend and that they'll be happy at, knowing that if they don't make the team, they can still participate in intramural sports. Most students should not sacrifice their ability to attend a very good school just because they want to play sports. People should attend the best school, from an academic standpoint, that they possibly can.

CHAPTER

GET A DATE

MAKING THE ROMANCE CONNECTION, AND THEN SOME

omantic relationships are certainly part of the college experience, whether you will be continuing a high school romance or searching for a new love. If you plan on maintaining a long-distance romance with your high school boyfriend/girlfriend, that'll take a bit of trust, patience, and planning and a lot of extra money to support your long-distance phone bills. (To save money on phone bills, use e-mail and limit your calls to only a few times per week.)

Needless to say, if you've decided to maintain a long-distance relationship with someone from your high school years, one of the keys to the success of that relationship will be staying faithful, despite the fact that you'll be in an environment filled with new prospects. Knowing that you'll be faithful to your boyfriend/girlfriend, and he or she will be faithful to you will help maintain the bond you have for each other. If a basic trust does not exist between you, and you probably won't have the opportunity to see your high school boyfriend/girlfriend, except on vacations, you should seriously consider where the relationship is headed.

If you're totally single and looking for romance, your college years will provide you with countless opportunities. Now that you're at school, you'll quickly discover that for the first time in your life, you have many freedoms that you didn't have while living at home. For example, you have no curfew, you can have people of the opposite sex in your bedroom whenever you want, and you don't have to be worried about getting caught doing things that you don't want your parents (or siblings) knowing about.

With these new freedoms comes a tremendous amount of responsibility! We're living in an age where sexually transmitted diseases like AIDS are realities, and dangers that face EVERYONE. As a result, it is your responsibility to take precautions and practice safe sex in every aspect of your physical relationship. Unfortunately, even if you're not experiencing sexual intercourse with your boyfriend/girlfriend, if you are intimate, there is a chance of being exposed to a sexually transmitted disease. Before getting physical, you must be

On a more cheerful note, meeting someone new and dating him or her can be a wonderful experience filled with good times. Even if you're on a tight budget and can't afford fancy dates or romantic getaways, you can still have a fun-filled relationship while in school. Here are some ideas for fun dates:

- Take romantic walks.
- Go hiking.
- Rollerblade (in-line skate).
- Take bike rides.
- Go to movies.
- Rent videos in your dorm.
- Have a romantic picnic at a local park.
- Hang out at a local coffee house.
- Attend a football game together and support your college's team.
- Visit a tourist attraction in the city your school is in (visit a museum, aquarium, historical sight, planetarium, etc.).
- Go to a concert or show.
- Order a pizza and hang out in the dorm.
- Play a board game.
- Walk around a mall.
- Go ice skating.
- Go to a dance club, nightclub, or comedy club.

responsible and learn about your partner's sexual history.

If you're planning on playing the field while in school, keep in mind that no news travels faster then gossip. Knowing this, treat people with respect. If you want to break off a relationship, be mature about it. Always be open and honest with the people you're dating. Avoid playing mind games. Obviously, you're not going to fall in love with everyone you go out on a date with. If you discover after one or two dates there is no "love connection," don't lead the other person on or simply blow him or her off by never calling again. If you treat the other person with respect, you could wind up with a new friend. Besides, that person could have a friend that's more compatible with you.

When it comes to dating, image is important. Try to convey a positive visual image of yourself. Just to be on the safe side, suck on a breath mint early in the evening (or after eating), and don't forget to put on deodorant. You could easily work up a sweat on the dance floor.

Your college years will provide you with what could ultimately be one of the best opportunities to meet new people. Don't be afraid to take advantage of this opportunity and participate in social events at your school. If you're a shy person, you may have to work extra hard to strike up conversations and become an active participant in activities that interest you. The harder you try at the beginning, the more successful you'll ultimately be, and the easier meeting new people will become. Also, don't be afraid to ask your friends if they know people you could date. Networking is a wonderful way of meeting new people, and although it runs against the popular mythology, blind dates can be fun.

And, ladies, we're almost in the twenty-first century! Don't be afraid to approach a guy and ask him out on a date, or to arrange for a mutual friend to make an introduction for you, or to set up a group date so you can get to know the person you're interested in without the pressure of a one-on-one date. When you're part of the dating scene, it's important to keep an open mind. Everyone has preconceived notions of their "dream guy" or "dream girl," but you must be willing to be flexible rather than only dating people that fit exactly into what you perceive as the perfect person for you from a looks, intelligence, or personality standpoint.

What Exactly Is Safe Sex Anyway?

Safe sex refers to two things: the prevention of pregnancy and the prevention of sexually transmitted diseases (including HIV). Obviously, the safest way to avoid getting pregnant or catching a sexually transmitted disease is to refrain from having sex. Although women can become pregnant as a result of having sexual intercourse, men and women (and you too) can catch sexually transmitted diseases.

There is always a risk of pregnancy or catching a sexually transmitted disease as a result of having sexual intercourse: No method of contraception is 100-percent effective. It's also possible to transmit (or receive) a sexually transmitted disease through oral sex. Some experts even believe kissing is a way such diseases can be transmitted from one person to another.

If you are going to experience any type of intimacy with another person, it's an excellent idea for you both to see a doctor or be tested for sexually transmitted diseases BEFORE you are intimate. Since anything and everything you discuss with a medical doctor is totally private, feel free to ask any type of sex-related question(s) about anything that you don't fully understand. A doctor is also the ideal person to talk to about methods of birth control and the prevention of sexually transmitted diseases. For many people, discussing these topics can be extremely embarrassing, but if you think you're responsible enough to experience sexual relations with another person, then you must be sure you're also well informed. If you feel intimidated discussing these topics with your doctor, then find yourself another doctor. Don't rely on infor-

mation from friends, your sexual partner, or even books dedicated to the subject. Discuss all of your options with a doctor!

Having the right information and acting responsibly can mean the difference between life and death—literally! Don't think HIV or AIDS is something that other people get and that it can't happen to you. Guess what...it can! Every single person who has ever had any type of sexually transmitted disease has thought that it could never happen to them.

Just because birth control exists, it doesn't mean that you should be having sex. There are many ways of being intimate with your boyfriend or girlfriend without experiencing sexual intercourse. Whether or not you choose to have sex before you're married is an extremely personal and emotional decision that's based on your own moral values and often your religious beliefs. Whatever you do, never decide to have sex as a result of pressure from your boyfriend or girlfriend, or as a result of pressure from your friends. Wait until you and your potential partner are emotionally ready to experience sexual intercourse; you'll know when the time is right.

Whose Responsibility Is Birth Control—the Guy's or the Girl's?

Birth control and safe sex precautions are the responsibility of both partners. Both the guy and the girl should insist on using protection BEFORE engaging in any form of sexual relations. If your partner refuses to use some form of protection, he or she probably shouldn't be your partner (that is, unless you're already married or you're trying to have a baby).

Methods of Birth Control

Especially for females, choosing to use contraception and then deciding which form of contraception to use is a highly personal decision that has both emotional and medical ramifications. Be sure to consult a doctor or medical expert for the latest information and failure rates for each form of contraception, and make sure that you have a complete understanding of how the method of contraception you choose should be used. Since the use of contraception is also a religious decision for some people, you might also consider seeking the advice from a priest, rabbi, or other religious leader.

The following brief descriptions of most of the birth control methods available. These descriptions have been provided by the Department of Health and Human Services Public Health Service and the Food and Drug Administration (FDA).

Condoms

For many people, the prevention of STDs, including HIV, which leads to AIDS, is a factor in choosing a contraceptive. Only one form of birth control—the latex condom—is considered to be highly effective in helping protect against

HIV and other STDs. Condoms protect both the male and the female from STDs, plus help to prevent pregnancy as a result of sexual intercourse. A male condom is a sheath that covers the penis during sex.

Condoms are made of either latex rubber or natural skin (called "lambskin," which is actually manufactured using sheep intestines). Of these two types, ONLY LATEX CONDOMS have been show to be highly effective in helping to prevent STDs. Each condom can only be used one time. (Never attempt to recycle them by washing them and then reusing them.) Condoms have a birth control failure rate of about fifteen percent. However, most failures can be traced to improper use.

When you go to the convenience store or pharmacy to purchase condoms, you'll see that you have many choices. Some condoms have spermicide added. This may offer some additional protection against pregnancy. Some condoms also have lubricants added. Non-oil-based lubricants can also be used with condoms. Oil-based lubricants, such as petroleum jelly (Vaseline), should NEVER be used with a condom, because it will weaken the latex.

Condoms are relatively cheap, easy to use, and readily available. Supermarkets, pharmacies, convenience stores, many gas stations, and even your college bookstore most likely sell condoms. They can also be purchased from vending machines at nightclubs and bars, obtained from your school's medical center, or even bought via mail order. Once again, if you're old enough to be experiencing sexual relations, you must be responsible enough to purchase some form of protection for yourself and your partner. When purchasing a condom (for yourself or your partner) use common sense. Buy name-brand condoms. You might pay more, but it's worth it. Also, you'll notice that condoms come in several sizes. Guys, don't act macho and buy a condom that doesn't fit your personal equipment. The sex experts say that the size of your equipment doesn't matter, but the size of your condom does. It is critical that the condom should fit, as they say, like a glove.

Female Condom

This type of contraceptive was approved by the FDA in April 1993. It consists of a lubricated polyurethane sheath with a flexible polyurethane ring on each end. One ring is inserted into the vagina, much like a diaphragm, and the other remains outside, partially covering the labia.

Periodic Abstinence

Periodic abstinence involves NOT having sexual intercourse during the woman's fertile period. This method is also called Natural Family Planning or the Rhythm Method. Using this method successfully is dependent on the ability to identify the approximately ten-day period in each menstrual cycle that a woman is fertile. This method may sound good, but it's level of failure can be as high as 47 percent, and that's if you do everything correctly. This method offers no protection from STDs.

Surgical Sterilization

Surgical sterilization is available to both males and females. However, the results are permanent, which means that having kids later in life will be out of the question. As a college student, this birth control method should not be one you consider, unless it's strongly advised by a doctor for medical reasons.

For women, tubal ligation seals the fallopian tubes so that an egg cannot travel to the uterus. For men, a vasectomy involves closing off a man's vas deferens so that sperm will not be carried to the penis. A vasectomy is considered safer than female sterilization.

Spermicides

Spermicides come in many forms, including foams, jellies, gels, and suppositories. Each form of spermicide works by building a physical and chemical barrier to sperm. The active ingredient in most spermicides is the chemical nonoxynol-9. The failure rate for spermicides in preventing pregnancy when used alone is from 20 to 30 percent. Some people experience burning or irritation as a result of using spermicides. If these side effects occur, stop using the spermicide immediately.

Diaphragm

This is a flexible rubber disk with a rigid rim. Diaphragms range in size from two to four inches in diameter and are designed to cover the cervix during and after intercourse. Spermicidal jelly or cream MUST be placed inside of the diaphragm for it to be effective against preventing unwanted pregnancy. A diaphragm must be fitted by a health professional and the correct size must be prescribed to insure a snug seal with the vaginal wall.

Cervical cap

The cervical cap is a dome-shaped rubber cap that fits snugly over the cervix. Like the diaphragm, it is used with a spermicide and must be fitted by a doctor or health care professional.

Hormonal contraception

Available only by prescription, hormonal contraception involves ways of delivering forms of two female reproductive hormones—estrogen and progestogen—that help regulate ovulation (release of an egg), the condition of the uterine lining, and other parts of the menstrual cycle. Hormones interact with the body, and have the potential for serious side effects, though this is rare. When properly used, hormonal methods are effective.

Birth control pills

There are two types of birth control pills: combination pills, which contain both estrogen and a progestin, and "mini-pills," which contain only progestin. The combination pill prevents ovulation; the mini-pill reduces cervical mucus and causes it to thicken, preventing the man's sperm from reaching the egg. Birth control pills can have serious side effects. Smokers and women with certain medical conditions should not take the pill. Be sure to discuss the possible drawbacks of using birth control pills with your doctor.

Norplant

First approved by the FDA in 1990, Norplant involves a minor surgical procedure on a female, during which six matchstick-sized rubber capsules containing progestin are placed just underneath the skin of the upper arm. The implant is effective within twenty-four hours and provides progestin for up to five years or until it is removed. Both the insertion and the removal of Norplant must be performed by a qualified professional. Because contraception is automatic, and does not depend on the user, the failure rate of Norplant is less than 1 percent for women who weigh less than 150 pounds. Women who weigh more have a higher pregnancy rate after the first two years. Women who cannot take birth control pills for medical reasons should not consider Norplant as a contraceptive option. Like most drugs, Norplant can cause unwanted side effects that can include headaches, irregular menstrual bleeding, depression, nausea, and acne. Norplant does not prevent sexually transmitted diseases, such as AIDS.

Depo-Provera

This form of contraception is an injectable form of progestin. It was approved by the FDA back in 1992 for contraceptive use. Depo-Provera is reported to have a failure rate of only 1 percent, and each injection provides contraception for fourteen weeks. It is injected every three months into a woman's buttocks or arm, and must be administered by a trained medical professional. Like Norplant, Depo-Provera

can cause unwanted side effects, and does not prevent STDs.

IUDs

These are small, plastic, flexible devices that are inserted into the woman's uterus through the cervix by a trained clinician. There are two types of IUDs that are marketed in the United States: ParaGard T380A, which is effective for eight years, and Progestasert, which is effective for one year, after which time they must be replaced. Both forms of IUDs have a 4 to 5 percent failure rate. IUDs are recommended mainly to women in mutually monogamous relationships.

More detailed information is available from a booklet called *Choosing a Contraceptive*, which is available, free of charge, from the Consumer Information Catalog. Write to the Consumer Information Center, P.O. Box 100, Pueblo, Colorado, 81002. If you have access to the Internet, you can also download this publication from the Consumer Information Catalog's Web site (http://www.pueblo.gsa.gov).

Some Important Facts about AIDS

Whether you're straight, gay, or bisexual, if you're going to be sexually active, then you must have a good understanding of what AIDS is and how it could ultimately kill you if you don't practice safe sex. HIV, the virus which causes AIDS, is contagious, but not in the same way that measles or chicken pox or the common cold are contagious. HIV/AIDS is a sexually transmitted, blood-borne disease that spreads from one person to another in the following ways:

o By sexual intercourse between a man and a woman, or between two men. The virus can be spread through vaginal, anal, or oral sex

o By sharing contaminated needles used to inject drugs

o By an infected woman to her baby during pregnancy or delivery, and possibly through breast-feeding

o By transfusion of contaminated blood or blood components, although this risk has been sharply reduced by screening blood and blood donors

Someone with HIV or AIDS might look totally healthy and show no signs of symptoms for years, which means that before engaging in sexual activities, you must know the truth about your partner's sexual history. If you're going to be intimate with your partner, you should both undergo AIDS tests prior to any sexual activities. An AIDS test can be done by any doctor, or you can now purchase a home test for under $50 from most local pharmacies or by mail order. To find out about the Confide home HIV/AIDS test, which is available from local pharmacies, call (800) THE-TEST.

Scientists have found no evidence that HIV is spread through casual non-sexual contact, by sharing meals or office equipment, or by handshakes or hugs with an infected person.

Thus, there is no reason to avoid normal, non-sexual, social contact with

someone who you know is infected with HIV.

The AIDS virus is not spread by sexual intercourse between two people who maintain a sexual relationship exclusively with each other and have not been previously infected. As a general rule, however, the best protection against sexually transmitted infection by the virus is to abstain from sex or have a mutually monogamous relationship with an uninfected person. Avoid sexual contact with people who have AIDS, people who have tested positive for the AIDS virus antibody, and people at a high risk of infection.

Unless you are absolutely 100 percent sure that your partner is not infected, avoid any and all contact with his or her blood, semen, urine, feces, saliva, and/or vaginal secretions. According to medical experts, the use of a condom will greatly enhance your protection against this virus. However, because there is still a lot to be learned about HIV and AIDS, no medical experts can guarantee that simply using a condom will provide 100 percent protection against the virus. This is why knowing your partner's sexual history is so important. It goes without saying that engaging in sexual activities with a prostitute could kill you if you become infected with HIV/AIDS.

At this time, there is no known cure for HIV/AIDS and no drug that can be used to prevent the virus. Thus, your only protection is to engage in safe sex (or no sex) and to become involved only in monogamous sexual relationships. There is absolutely no doubt that AIDS is deadly, so your survival depends on acting appropriately before having sex with a partner.

To learn more about AIDS, call the National AIDS Hotline at (800) 342-AIDS. Your call will be kept confidential.

For additional information about human immunodeficiency virus (HIV), acquired immunodeficiency syndrome (AIDS), and other socially transmitted diseases (STDs), you can call the Center for Disease Control (CDC) National HIV & AIDS Hotline at (800) 342-2437 or (800) 344-7432 (Spanish). This service is available twenty-four hours per day, seven days a week and is confidential. The CDC also has a hotline for information about STDs. Call (800) 227-8922 (weekdays between 8 a.m. and 11 p.m.). The National Herpes Hotline can be reached at (919) 361-8488 (long-distance charges will apply).

PART FOUR:

THE STUDY SCENE

CHAPTER

20

DEVELOPING GOOD STUDY HABITS

START OUT ON THE RIGHT FOOT

PARTY

STUDY

et's face it, college is about meeting new people, experiencing new things, being on your own for the first time, and learning. When you get right down to it, college is also about attending classes, reading textbooks, writing papers, and doing lots of studying. Knowing how to manage your time and studying correctly will not only provide you with plenty of extra hours per week that you can spend doing fun things but also help to ensure that you earn the best possible grades. This chapter will help you develop important study habits that you should begin applying in your early days as a freshman.

It's all too easy to become so caught up in the details that you lose sight of what you are studying and why. Without a sense of this big picture, you can easily feel unfocused. However, if you maintain a clear sense of what you are doing and why, you are more likely to remain on track. Throughout your studies, as you become immersed in the details of various subjects and tasks, make certain that you step back every so often to appreciate that big picture. Try to see how each task you go about fits into it. If you see how each task contributes something of use to you personally, you'll remain much more focused on your work; you'll also find your studies more fulfilling.

Passive Versus Active Studying

Although they don't realize it, many students approach studying as a passive activity. They think that as long as they look at their notes and read their textbooks they are covering the material adequately. Studying, in this sense, is not much different from watching television: You simply look, listen, and somehow "take it all in." But you probably are

never going to have an exam on a particular television show.

The material you study in school, though, is different; you will be tested on it and need to recall information in great detail. Moreover, you will often need to take information you've learned and apply it to other areas. Sitting back and "taking it all in" is therefore not going to cut it.

Rather than approaching studying in this passive manner, this chapter emphasizes the importance of active study. Active studying means you do something. Instead of merely looking at and listening to new material, you think about it and, in the process, make it a part of your general knowledge. As a result, you are better able to remember the information for exams and also to apply it to other situations.

In a general sense, you need to establish yourself as an active student right from the start. That means acknowledging that your education involves work—hard work. Even though you might be sitting at a desk or lying on the couch reading over notes, your mind must remain hard at work. As soon as you slip into a passive mode, the material before you will be lost and you might as well have been watching television.

IMPORTANT POINTS TO REMEMBER

1. Always keep sight of the big picture; remember why you are in school and what you hope to gain.
2. Set short-term and long-term goals for yourself.
3. Be an active student, not a passive one.
4. Think of studying as communicating—with teachers, texts, fellow students, and yourself.

Live and In Person

The point of taking notes is not to have a copy of what the teacher has told you. If that were the case, why would there be lectures at all? Wouldn't it just be easier to read it in a book? The fact is that live communication is very powerful and very effective. For example, if you were to try to have a telephone conversation with someone who spoke Swahili, it would be impossible for you to understand what was being said (unless, of course, you happen to speak it yourself). However, if you were to try to have the conversation in person, you'd probably understand something. You'd be able to read body language, watch gestures, and pay attention to facial expressions, which provide information about what is being communicated. In turn, the speaker would see from your expression what you did and did not understand and adopt other techniques to try to communicate.

By attending live lectures, you can gain a deeper understanding of the material being presented. As in a conversation with someone who speaks another language, you'll receive additional information through body lan-guage, expression, and tone of voice. Also, simply by being present and listening attentively, you'll pick up more of the material than you would be merely reading. Live performance, after all, is generally more compelling and likely to hold your interest; that's why people pay so much for concert and theater tickets.

By the Way, You Should Leave the Tape Recorder at Home

Some students think they'll take the easy way out by bringing a tape recorder to class, and relying on that instead of taking notes. However, the tape recorder ultimately means much more work. The students get home and have all that tape to sit through, which means, in effect, going to class twice.

By taking notes in class, you're already beginning to digest and to edit the information. For example, you might not write down information that you already know or have taken notes on previously. You also don't need to write down the detailed explanations your professor makes to recall and understand a particular concept. Since your notes are succinct, they will take far less time to read over than it would take to listen to an entire lecture on tape again.

Then there's the problem of mechanical difficulties. Tape recorders are machines. What if the batteries run out or the tape doesn't record well and you can't hear what the teacher said? What if the tape gets eaten? Minimize these risks by leaving the tape recorder at home.

There is one way that a tape recorder may help you. If you must miss a lecture for some reason, you might want to have a friend record it so you'll be able to keep up. Make certain, though, that you listen to the lecture and take notes just as if you were sitting in class. It's also a good idea to do this before the next class so you can keep up with the course.

BE A PACKRAT:
YOU NEVER KNOW WHAT YOU'LL NEED AGAIN

Many students are so relieved when the semester is over they throw away all their notes. That's a serious mistake. You've worked hard taking those notes. And, more important, you never know when you might need to refer back to them.

Many of the courses you take will interconnect, particularly those within your major or concentration. As you move on to more advanced levels, you'll find you need to refer to notes from earlier courses to refresh your memory about certain key points.

You also may take courses that seem completely unrelated to one another, only to find that some point or issue will come up that you have previously addressed. For example, you may be reading a novel in an English class that refers to specific historical events. If you've taken a history class about that period, you can read your notes and get more information about those events, which in turn can help you understand the novel. Imagine how impressed your teacher will be if, in class discussion, you can provide some of that background information.

At the end of the semester, rather than throwing away all your notes, neatly label and put them someplace safe and accessible. Consider purchasing a file cabinet to store them in. If you've been using a loose-leaf notebook (as recommended earlier), you can take the pages out of the binder and put them in a folder. That way you can reuse the binder next semester. Just make certain you label the folder with the course title and year. A file cabinet will help keep everything organized.

In addition to saving old notes, consider holding onto some of your required textbooks and other course materials. It's tempting at the end of the semester to sell all your books back to the bookstore—especially given how expensive books are these days. However, if there is any chance you will refer to a book—particularly if it was used in a course that is part of your major—it is probably worthwhile to hold onto it. One option is to sell only the textbooks and hold onto all other books. Textbooks tend to be more expensive than other books, and you get back a significant amount of money. Other books often bring only a fraction of the original cost (especially if they are paperbacks). If you sell one of these but wind up having to purchase it again, you actually lose rather than save money!

Learning to Listen

Taking effective notes doesn't start when you begin writing; it begins with being an effective listener. We take it for granted that we all know how to listen, that listening is a natural skill requiring no work at all. The truth is, listening is a difficult task and very few people know how to do it well. Have you ever been in the midst of a conversation with someone, nodding your head in agreement, and suddenly found yourself unable to respond to a question they've just asked? Although you may have heard him, you weren't listening to him.

Why is listening so difficult? One reason is that we confuse hearing with listening. Hearing is passive; it means some sound has reverberated in your ear, whether or not you want it to, and there's been a noise. Listening, on the other hand, is an active process. It implies that you must do something to accomplish it. It takes action and, often, work to listen well. For example, let's say you are sitting on a crowded train talking with a friend. You hear the noise of the train, the chatter of passengers around you, the boom box being blasted by a teenager, and, somewhere in all that, you even hear your friend. But to under-stand what your friend is telling you, you need to do something; you need to listen to distinguish her words from all the background noise.

The same principle applies to class-room lectures. There may not be the same amount of noise in a lecture room as on a crowded train (although there is plenty of distracting racket, from feet shuffling to heaters blowing), but you still have to work hard to listen to the pro-fessor's words.

Following are strategies for effective listening. They can help with your note taking as well as with any interpersonal encounters, from conversations to job interviews. Develop good listening skills now and they'll last a lifetime and con-tinue to bring you success. People respect someone who listens carefully. More important, those who listen are certain to catch important information that others don't.

Strategies for Effective Listening

1. *Make the effort.* The first step to effective listening is to realize that listening takes effort. It won't

happen on its own and it's not something that is going to take place naturally, just by your being there. Go into situations where it's important for you to listen determined to listen, and listen carefully. Concentrate. It may be difficult at first, but in time you'll get better.

2. *Pay attention to the speaker.* It is very difficult to listen to someone if you are not giving all your attention to that person. Ideally, you should look at the person's face the entire time she is speaking. However, in a lecture this is not always possible because you also need to look at your notes from time to time. Try, if you can, to write while keeping your eye on the professor. This may make your notes more messy than usual but, in time, you'll get more adept at writing without looking at the page. If you can't write and look at the professor at the same time, make certain to look up from your notes frequently. This will insure that you are maintaining a direct line of communication with her.

If the professor is explaining a difficult concept, you are much better off not writing and looking only at her. This way, you can concentrate on listening and understanding. After the professor is finished, jot down a few notes or phrases to help you remember what was said.

3. *Minimize distraction.* To maintain that direct line of communication between you and the speaker, it's important to minimize all outside distractions. Different things can be distracting. Perhaps there's someone very attractive who you always sit near in class and who occupies more of your attention than the professor. Maybe a friend you sit with can't resist chatting during the lecture. Even something as tame as chewing gum or a grumbling stomach can begin to sound like a major earthquake when you are trying to pay attention to something else. Choose your seat carefully and come to class well-fed and prepared to listen.

You might also decide to sit closer to the professor if it helps you concentrate better. Sitting in the first few rows is not absolutely crucial; in fact, some people feel very uncomfortable being that close to the professor. However, if you are having trouble hearing or concentrating, try sitting in the first or second row. You might be surprised at how much more of the lecture you catch.

Additionally, the way you sit can also affect your ability to pay attention. If you slouch in the chair, your eyes won't be focused on the speaker. Each time you want to look at the teacher, you will have to lift up your entire head, and the effort needed to do that can disrupt your note taking. Instead, it is much more effective to sit with your back against the chair back. Place the sheet of paper in the center of the desk and hold it in place with whichever hand you do not use to write. If you sit in this position, you should be able to watch the professor while writing; you also will be able to glance down at your notes by just moving your eyes, not your entire head.

4. *Watch for lapses.* Become more attuned to the times when your mind is drifting to other subjects or your eyes are wandering out of the window. When this happens, focus your attention back on the speaker immediately. Be aware that everyone is prone to lapses in attention, and that if you can recognize when your mind wanders, you will begin to correct yourself much faster and not miss as much.

5. *Work at it.* Listening, like any skill, improves as you work at it. As you try to concentrate in different situations, you'll find you get better and better at it.

6. *Watch for clues from the speaker.* Listening effectively means more than paying attention to the words of the speaker. People convey a great deal of information through the way they speak as well as what they say. Get in the habit of concentrating on additional signals from a speaker besides spoken words. Pay attention to the speaker's tone of voice, the volume of their speech, pauses, hand gestures, and body language—these signals can enhance your understanding of the speaker's words. Additionally, by being alert to these elements in addition to spoken words, you have more to occupy your attention, insuring that you remain actively engaged in the lecture, conversation, or discussion.

CHAPTER

21

THE DAILY GRIND

GETTING THE MOST OUT OF YOUR CLASSES

Taking Notes in Class

Make Preparations

Developing good study habits requires that you combine multiple skills, such as time management, reading, writing, and reviewing. Your class notes and notes that you take based on your reading will prove as important if not more important than the textbook for that class. Thus, you must learn how to determine what's important when you're reading a textbook or listening to a lecture, and then understand how to translate key pieces of information into your notes and ultimately into your memory. Your ability to take complete and organized notes will prove to be extremely valuable during your entire college experience.

When you get to class, take out a new sheet of paper. You may have brought the notes from the previous class with you, but you should always start each class with a fresh piece of paper. This is because lectures tend to have their own separate topics or themes.

Always put the date and subject at the top of the first sheet, so you can put them in the proper binder or section at home. Next, you should draw a line down the page about three inches from the left,

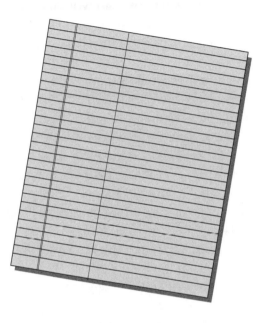

so that you have an extra-wide margin. Your paper will then look like this:

During class, take notes only on the right side of the margin. Leave the left side totally blank—you'll be using that space when you get to stage two, working on notes at home. You should also take notes on only one side of the paper; the back side will be used later.

Write Down All Key Terms

The first and foremost commandment of note taking is this: You cannot write down everything the professor says. Your next question probably is, So what exactly am I supposed to write down?

In taking notes, your aim should not be to create an exact transcript of the professor's lecture. If that were the case, the professor would simply hand out photocopies. Writing down information and concepts that are new and unfamiliar should be your priority.

During lectures, the main thing professors do is communicate new information. The majority of it is specific, such as names of people or places, significant dates, certain theories, formulas, and concepts. These are the key terms of the lecture. A goal of note taking, then, is to keep track of all these key terms.

As you take down these key terms in class, don't worry about their correct spelling or pronunciation. Just write out words the way they sound. Try to be as accurate as possible. Later on, you can find out the right way to spell them. Believe it or not, if you write down just these key terms, you'll have a pretty accurate representation of the entire lecture.

Avoid Complete Sentences

There's no reason why your notes have to be written in complete, grammatically correct sentences. Sentences are filled with words that aren't necessary for one to understand the gist of them. You can still understand the basic meaning of a sentence without using all the words in it. For example, you can leave out articles (the, a, an) and pronouns (he, she, they, it) and still understand the basic information.

Construct a Rough Outline

The key terms we've been discussing don't exist in isolation; instead, they are part of a larger structure. Each term ties in to some bigger topic or point being addressed in the professor's lecture. As you write down these other topics or points, you can begin to construct a rough outline that will help you see how various terms are related and the topics they refer to.

Don't get stressed out at the idea of making an outline. You may be thinking that outlines are real headaches, that they are overly complicated and don't help all that much. The reason you feel that way is probably because you've been taught that there's only one way to make an outline and that it's a complex matter, with Roman numerals and letters. You don't have to worry about any of that. A rough outline for your notes can consist of a simple diagram that helps you to keep track of how various points and topics are related.

Note General Themes

As we have just noted, each lecture has a main topic and various subtopics. There might also be certain points, issues, and concepts that come up again and again within a single class and throughout the term. These are probably very important and should be noted.

It is also important that, at the end of each class, you take a few moments to jot down the major themes—the major topics and key points your professor made—from that day's lecture. Write these down as soon after the lecture has ended as possible, when the lecture is still fresh in your mind. Keeping track of these helps a great deal in preparation for exams. As a semester progresses, you'll begin to notice patterns in the lectures as certain themes recur. Very often, these themes are the major focus of examinations.

Ask yourself these questions: What were the major points the teacher made? What were the main topics? Try to pay particular attention to any opinions or stances about the material your professor might have conveyed to you. What seems to be the professor's personal opinion about the material? What does the professor seem to care about the most?

Note Taking Outside of Class

You might be asking yourself the questions, Aren't we done with note taking already? Most students don't open their notebooks again until exam time, only to find they can't make sense out of much of what they've written. This produces a last-minute panic before the exam, as students struggle to relearn an entire semester's worth of material in a few days. Instead of waiting until the last minute to figure out what you've in your notes, get in the habit of working with them outside of the classroom.

Read Over Your Notes

Read your notes over at least once outside of class. This will serve two very important purposes: It will give you an opportunity to clarify anything that might be confusing, and it will help you learn the information. It also helps you develop a comfortable familiarity with the whole subject.

If you continue reading over your notes, you'll become more and more immersed in your subject. When the exam comes, you'll feel like you have the information well at hand. Questions won't shock you because they seem alien; instead, they will elicit more educated responses.

Make reading over your notes a part of your study habits. You don't need to spend a great deal of time doing this—one or two hours a week per subject should be plenty of time. It's a good idea to do this on Friday or the weekend, so you can look at all your notes for the week. You don't have to read over your notes each night; in fact, you're better off leaving them alone for a few days. That way, you can approach them with a fresh mind.

Ask Yourself Questions

Don't read over your notes with a passive eye. You won't learn anything if you simply read without thinking about what you are reading. Instead, become as involved in your notes as you can. You can do this by considering these questions as you read:

- What does this mean? Does it make sense?
- How are these terms and topics related to one another?
- How do these terms and topics fit into the big picture?

Take Notes on Your Notes

If you draw a line down each page about three inches from the left so you have an extra-wide margin, you can use this space to take notes on your notes. As you ask yourself the questions just listed, jot down answers here. If something confuses you, make a note of it.

You can also begin to make connections between various topics and terms in this space. During class, you might have tried to put your notes in a rough outline form. As you read over them, other relationships might become clear. No longer in the middle of a lecture, you now have a sense of the whole topic. You know where your professor is heading with the material. You have a better sense of what information is important and what doesn't matter as much. Jot down these thoughts in that left-hand margin. Remember also to only take notes on one side of the page in class so that you can use the back side to jot down additional notes if you run out of room in the left-hand column.

Go to Other Sources

When you're finished reading over your notes, you should mark areas or write down things that confuse you. Rather than letting those things go and praying they won't be on an exam, you should take the time to figure them out.

Many people assume that the only source for information for class notes is the professor. That means you are entirely dependent on that one person for all the information. That's not fair to the professor and it's not fair to you. No one can communicate everything in a way that's entirely clear to every person. And as we've noted, some professors are much better at communicating than others. At the same time, you have to take some responsibility for your own education. You can't just sit back and rely on someone else to do all the work for you.

So, if something confuses you, try to educate yourself. There are several places where you can get help, and you can usually get it quickly and easily.

Borrow a Friend's Notes: No two people take exactly the same notes. There's a good chance that something you missed during a lecture was caught by someone else. If you missed some information or don't understand a section of your notes, look at a friend's notes. There's absolutely nothing wrong with sharing notes with a friend. Just make certain the friend is a reliable note taker. You don't want to borrow notes from someone who doesn't take decent notes; you might wind up copying down incorrect information. However, if you know someone who seems like a smart student and efficient note taker, you can exchange notes on a regular basis.

Check Your Textbook: Your textbook for the course and any other required reading materials are valuable resources. Very often, the required reading assignments you do outside of class correspond to the lectures. These may cover many of the same topics and key terms discussed in the lecture. In a lecture, your comprehension is dependent on your listening skills, but in a textbook, where there is a written explanation laid out on the page, you have plenty of time to make sense of the material.

Check the index of the textbook for a listing of the topic or key term for which you want more information. The text's discussion of it may not necessarily be in the same chapter you read for homework. By checking the index, you'll be able to see all the pages in the book where the term is mentioned. For all you know, there is an excellent definition and description of a term in a chapter that's not assigned for homework.

Fill in Additional Information

As you go about your additional research, make certain you take notes and fill in missing information in your notebook. If you found an explanation or definition that helps, write it in your notes. Use the space on the left side of the margin or the back of the sheet. You can also take notes on additional sheets and add them to the notes for that day's lecture in your loose-leaf notebook.

IMPORTANT POINTS TO REMEMBER

1. Effective note taking starts with effective listening.
2. You don't have to write down everything the teacher says; in fact, you shouldn't even try to.
3. Notes aren't finished when you leave the classroom; you should continue working with them and thinking about them. This will help you learn the material and save time studying for exams later on.
4. You don't need to rely on what the teacher says as your only source of information; feel free to consult other sources for additional information or to clarify points that confuse you.
5. Develop your own shorthand for taking notes quickly. Just make certain your notes make sense to you.
6. Maintain a sense of the overall topic of each lecture and note general themes.

Becoming an Active Reader

One of the reasons taking notes during lectures is difficult is because people tend to be passive listeners. Well, being a passive reader is just as much of a problem.

You probably think that when you sit down, open a book, and read, you will absorb it all. In actuality, you can read every word on the page and not understand a bit of it. In order to become an effective reader, you have to be an active reader. That means doing more than just looking at the words on the page; it means becoming involved with the material and thinking while you read.

These are the basic steps for becoming an effective reader:

1. Know where you're headed— and why.
2. Make a rough outline.
3. Watch for key terms and take notes with brief definitions.
4. Note general themes.
5. Write a response.

Effective Reading: A Step-By-Step Strategy

Much of the reading you will be required to do in school will be in textbooks— books that are specifically written to be used for educational purposes. In many courses, you will also be required to read other materials, such as various kinds of books and articles. Although the following section specifically refers to reading a chapter of a textbook, the basic step-by-step strategy outlined here can be applied to just about anything you read for school.

Know Where You're Headed— and Why

When you go on a trip, you usually have a destination in mind and a route planned before you go. You know exactly where you are going and why—

and that's what keeps you from getting lost. The same holds true for reading. If you don't want your mind to wander, make certain you know right from the beginning where you're headed and the route you are taking.

Before you begin reading, think a bit about what you are reading. What is the title of the chapter, article, or text? Does it give you any hint as to what you can expect? As with classroom lectures, each chapter or article you read will have a main topic. Make certain you know the topic before you start to read.

Next, try to get a sense of the chapter's contents. Glance through the chapter and look at the various headings and subheadings of different sections. Look at the pictures, diagrams, and charts. Try to get a sense of what topics are included within a chapter, how they relate to one another, and how they come together within the main topic.

Keeping the "big picture" in mind as you read will help keep you on track. You'll have a sense of how each section fits into the overall text, and you'll know how much more material you have ahead of you, which can help you plan your time. Also, a sense of the chapter's contents can help you read more selectively.

Try to keep in mind not only what you are reading, but why. Of course, one

reason is because the material is required reading. But if that is the only reason, you are going to get bored pretty quickly. Each chapter should somehow contribute to your understanding of the course material, as well as to your general knowledge. If you can designate a purpose for each thing you read, you'll feel better about doing the work. You won't be reading just to please the professor, but because you see some value in fulfilling the assignment.

Think about some of these questions:

○ What do you think your professor is hoping you will gain by reading this?
○ What might you personally gain from reading this?
○ How does the chapter or text fit in with the overall subject matter of the course?
○ How does the text fit in with the current course topics (i.e., the lectures for that week)?
○ Does the chapter build on previous material? How?
○ Does the chapter prepare you for upcoming topics? How?
○ Is anything in the chapter familiar to you? What? Where and when did you first learn it? What did you already learn? What in the chapter is new to you?

Thinking about these questions will help you become actively involved in the reading assignment right from the start. Contemplating these issues helps you evaluate how important the assignment is to you, which will also help you be a selective reader. These questions also help you gain a more personal interest in the reading by connecting it with your overall knowledge. That way, you won't feel you are reading just because it's required, but because it can somehow enhance your understanding of the subject matter.

Make a Rough Outline

Just as you do when taking notes during a lecture, you should make a rough outline of all reading assignments. This will fulfill two important purposes. First, taking notes will give you something to do while you read, making you more of an active reader with a purpose. This, in turn, will keep you focused on the assignment and minimize the tendency to let your mind wander. Second, these outlines will help you remember the material. When it comes time to study for an exam, you can read over these notes rather than have to go over large, highlighted chunks of text.

To make the rough outline, you merely need to note various topics and subtopics. You'll find that making an outline will be easier than taking notes during a lecture. Most textbooks, unlike most professors, are very clearly organized. Many books list, either in the table of contents or at the start of the chapter beneath the title, the topics covered in a particular chapter. Within a chapter, the topics, subtopics, and sub-subtopics usually have clearly labeled headings and subheadings. Most books differentiate between the more important topics and the lesser ones by changing the typeface style of the headings. For example, the more important headings will be larger and/or in boldface; less important ones will be smaller and in lighter or italic type.

As you read, watch for headings and subheadings and, as they come up, write them down. As with any outline, the less important a topic is, the more you indent it on your paper.

Watch for Key Terms and Take Notes with Brief Definitions

Most textbook chapters center on key terms—names, dates, facts, theories, formulas, and concepts—that are new to you. And just as you take notes in lectures, you should look for the key terms and include them in your reading notes. It will probably be easier to identify these terms in textbooks than during lectures because in most textbooks they are in boldface or italics. Try to fit them into your rough outline by placing them beneath the same heading or subheading in your notes as they appear in the chapter.

You should also try to include brief definitions of the key terms. You don't need to write these definitions in complete sentences. Use the same shorthand you would for taking lecture notes. As

with your lecture notes, you don't need to write in complete sentences or worry about grammar and punctuation. Feel free to use abbreviations and symbols. Just remember, though, that the notes should be easy for you to read. Don't copy down the word-for-word explanation of the term as you find it in the text. Instead, use your own words to define the term as briefly as possible. If, as you read over your notes later on, you don't understand something, you can always refer back to the textbook.

Note General Themes

When you are finished with a chapter, you should take a few minutes to jot down its general themes. To help you identify these, you might consider these questions:

- ○ What seemed to be the author's main concerns in this chapter?
- ○ What ideas, topics, or points were mentioned more than once?
- ○ Was there any kind of introduction or conclusion? If so, what points did the author make here?
- ○ Did you get a sense of the author's opinion or stance on the material he or she was addressing? What was it?

These notes will be instrumental in helping you prepare for exams. In addition to helping you recall the overall content of a reading assignment, they will enable you to compare the key themes of all the reading assignments and classroom lectures. This will help you gain a sense of how various parts of the course fit together. And it's a safe bet that when themes show up throughout the semester, they're likely to appear on an exam.

Write a Response

The reading process doesn't have to end when you get to the last word of the chapter. When they get to the last sentence of a reading assignment, most students think, "Whew! That's finished. What a relief!" and close the book without giving it another thought. They don't realize that a great deal of the work they've just done will have been a waste of time. While they have read the assignment, they have not really thought about it. They have looked at the words on the page, but they haven't thought about what they mean. They don't know if they even understood what they have just read. In short, they haven't really learned anything based on what they've read.

If you want to learn something from what you read, it is crucial that you think about it after you've finished reading. An excellent way to keep you thinking is to write a reading response. To write a reading response, you simply write whatever you want about what you've read.

First, close the book and put it aside, and take out a few sheets of fresh paper. Draw a line down the page so that you have a left-hand margin of about three inches. Write your response only on the right side of the margin; you'll use the space on the left-hand side later on.

A reading response is not a summary of the chapter. Instead, it's your opportunity to engage with the material you've just read. Think of yourself as having a conversation with the author of the text. This is your chance to share whatever is on your mind.

Here are some questions you might address in your response:

○ What is your emotional reaction to what you've read? Do you like what you read? Why or why not? How did reading the text make you feel? How do you think the writer wants you to feel?

○ What points do you think are most important to the writer? Did the writer successfully convey these to you?

○ What parts, if any, did you have trouble understanding? Why? What made it confusing?

○ What questions about the text do you still have? Make certain you list questions about any terms, topics, or points you didn't understand. You can also list questions you have that arise from the reading. Are there additional questions about the subject matter that were not addressed in the text? By the way, these questions don't necessarily have to be answered right away. They may be answered as you read more throughout the semester; or, they may never be answered.

○ How does this text connect with other things you've learned? Does it tie into things you've studied in other courses? Does the reading remind you of anything else?

These are just suggestions of topics you can address in your response. When you sit down to do the reading response, let yourself write whatever comes into your head. Set a time limit during which you will write about the assignment without stopping. You can set a limit of five or ten minutes per assignment.

CHAPTER 22

WRITING PAPERS
WHAT'S THE BIG IDEA?

Writing essays requires you to communicate back things you have learned. Both taking tests and writing essays center on how well you communicate.

Many people think writing is all about correct grammar and spelling. However, an essay can have flawless grammar and still not say anything. The essence of writing is communication. In any work of writing, you are communicating your ideas, thoughts, and beliefs to someone (or even yourself) in a way that makes them clearly understandable.

When you are immersed in writing an essay for class, you can easily forget that you are trying to communicate with a specific person—your teacher, who will grade the essay. However, you should always keep this in mind: What can you write that will most impress your teacher?

A teacher is probably not going to be overly impressed by flawless grammar and spelling; those qualities are expected. What will impress the teacher is the quality and strength of your ideas. Ideas are the crucial component of a good essay. They must be communicated in a manner that makes them accessible to the reader.

Coming up with sophisticated and intelligent ideas is your responsibility; no book can give them to you.

However, this chapter can teach you how to communicate those ideas in such a way that will show them off to their advantage. This chapter offers a step-by-step approach to writing essays that ensures your ideas are communicated in a clear, organized, and powerful manner. Following is a list of the eight steps involved in this approach:

1. Choose a general topic.
2. Read, think, and percolate.
3. Design a thesis statement.
4. Conduct research.
5. Jot down your own ideas.
6. Write the first draft.
7. Revise and redraft.
8. Do a final edit.

THE MATING HABITS OF THE MEDITERRANEAN TSETSE FLY

Choose a General Topic

To a large extent, the topic you choose determines how the final product will turn out. After all, an original and exciting topic will more likely result in an original and exciting essay. You should therefore not choose a topic haphazardly.

Your choice of topic must take into account the nature of the assignment and its requirements. Sometimes a teacher will assign a very specific topic and provide you with detailed requirements, specifying what the essay should address. However, even with the most rigidly defined assignment, you are going to have room to maneuver. In this case, the challenge is to view the subject from your own point of view and somehow to make it your own. You still need to spend time thinking about the assignment and how you plan to approach it in your own individual manner.

At other times, a teacher will suggest several topics or provide you with a very loosely defined assignment that gives you a great deal of freedom. Don't make the mistake of thinking that being allowed to choose your own topic makes the essay easier to write. Although having free rein with an essay is exciting, it can be over-whelming. There are so many possibilities for topics, how can you find one that's right for you?

What Interests You?

Choose a topic that, first and foremost, interests you. You are going to spend a great deal of time working on this essay, and if the topic itself doesn't ignite your interest, those hours will seem even longer and the writing process even more tedious. However, if you choose a subject you sincerely want to know more about, then the process of researching and writing the essay will be interesting and engaging.

Think about the various themes and topics that have been addressed in class, as well as the reading assignments you've completed. Was there a particular subject that you enjoyed learning about? Was there anything you only touched on in class that you wanted to know more about? Did you have an intense emotional reaction to anything? Do you have a particular opinion or point of view about a topic you'd like to express?

Consider Your Audience

In addition to considering your own interests, you do have to consider the teacher's expectations as well. Good writers always direct their work to the proper audience. For example, you would write a letter requesting a job interview in an entirely different manner than a love letter. In the case of a school essay, your audience will be the teacher who assigned it and will grade it. Before you begin work, make certain you understand the assignment, are aware of the teacher's expectations, and know the exact requirements for the essay. How much research should you be conducting? How long should the essay be? What format should you use? Is there anything specific you should include or address?

You might also want to choose a topic that your teacher will find unique. Many teachers become bored reading about the same topics over and over again; most will therefore welcome a paper written on something unusual. For example, if everyone else in the class is writing about a certain work of literature, then consider choosing a different one. Just make certain that your teacher is open to new ideas and atypical subjects. It may seem difficult to be original, especially if you are writing about a topic such as a historical event or literary work that has been discussed by others for centuries. However, the way you approach this topic can add a new twist to it that makes it seem original.

Too Long, Too Short, or Just Right?

In addition to considering your own interests and the instructor's expectations, consider the length requirements. Essays are meant to be detailed, in-depth studies of a particular subject. In order to write a solid, focused essay, you should choose a topic that can be addressed fully and comprehensively within the page requirements set by the teacher.

If you choose a topic that is too broad for the paper's length requirements, you will wind up writing about it in simplistic, superficial terms. You won't have the space to get into much detail, so the entire essay will remain on a broad and obvious level. For example, it would be difficult to write an essay on "The Poems of Emily Dickinson" in only six pages; you'd have to discuss each poem in one or two lines in order to get to them all. However, you could choose a more limited topic, such as a common theme in Dickinson's work, and address that in some depth.

Students often initially choose topics that are too broad because they are concerned about meeting the page requirements. At first, six or seven pages sounds like a lot to "fill up," so you might choose a huge topic to guarantee you have enough to write about. However, once you begin thinking about and researching your topic in depth, you'll find you have plenty of material. In fact, you may find you need to leave some material out.

Yet choosing a topic that is too limited for the page requirements is also a problem. If your topic is too narrow, you may find yourself bending over backward to meet the page requirements. Your paper then will be wordy and repetitive. For example, it would be difficult to come up with enough original ideas for a twenty-five-page essay on a single

Emily Dickinson poem; you would probably run out of material after the first few pages and repeat the same points over and over. Your topic should be broad enough so that you can fill the essay with strong ideas that keep the reader engaged.

Of course, you may not be able to settle on a specific topic right at the start. However, you don't need to. It's fine to begin with a broad, general topic and then gradually narrow it down until you hit upon a topic appropriate for the length of your essay.

A Place to Start

Here is a list of general topics that would make a good starting point for researching an essay:

- A particular work of literature, article, or text, or a body of works
- An author, person, or a particular group of individuals
- A historical period or event, or a contemporary news event
- A literary period or genre
- A scientific field or subfield, in either the general sciences or social sciences
- A particular issue or subject of debate, either historical or contemporary

All of the broad subjects listed would take lengthy papers to fully examine. However, they all make fine starting points for essays; you can choose one and begin to think and read more about it. As you do, you'll gradually be able to narrow it down to a topic appropriate for the length of your essay.

Read, Think, and Percolate

After you've chosen a general topic, you need to immerse yourself in the subject matter by reading and thinking about it at great length. By doing this, you learn more about the subject and can generate ideas to use in your essay. You also can begin to narrow the general topic down to a more specific one.

Start by reading anything you can find that relates to your chosen subject. The reference section of the library is an ideal place to begin reading. You can, for example, consult a general encyclopedia to see if there is an entry relating to your topic. Make certain you pick a thorough, academic encyclopedia such as *Encyclopaedia Britannica*, *Encyclopedia Americana*, or *Collier's Encyclopedia*. You can also find many spe-cialized dictionaries and encyclopedias that address specific fields. If you're having trouble finding a source, ask the reference librarian for suggestions.

Next, search the stacks of the library for general books on your topic. You can use the library's index (either the card catalog or a computerized index) and search according to the subject. Pick books that look promising and copy down their call numbers. All of the books related to that subject should be located in the same section of the library, so you can go to that section and browse. Select a few books that seem interesting and read sections of them. You don't necessarily need to read the entire book. For example, reading the introduction to a book on your topic may provide you with a great deal of information.

If you are writing an essay that centers on a specific text, such as a particular book or article, it is crucial that you reread that text several times. As you read, jot down any ideas that pop into your head that might make a contribution to an essay. Reading the text a few times may provide you with enough ideas to get started. However, if you find you are having difficulty, you may want to do some background reading to help you arrive at ideas of your own.

Don't expect the ideas to happen right away. The mind needs to let information percolate for a while. Soon, you'll begin making connections with things you've learned, forming your own opinions, and gaining insight into the material. As you continue reading, your ideas and interests will become more focused and defined, and you will be able to narrow down your topic. Although you don't have to concern yourself just yet with taking detailed notes, remember to make a brief note of any ideas that pop into your head.

Design a Thesis Statement

The key to any essay is its thesis statement. The thesis is the paper's central idea; it functions as the essay's backbone, holding together the various parts as a cohesive whole.

The thesis statement is not the same thing as your topic, although they are closely related. Your topic is a general subject that you've read and thought about to generate specific ideas. Based on that process, you should now be able to formulate a particular point of view about some aspect of the topic. This viewpoint, condensed into a single sentence that sums up the central idea of the essay, is your thesis statement.

Every essay should have a thesis statement, and all ideas expressed in the paper should reflect it. Without the thesis statement, the essay is merely a random list of ideas, without any clear, definable point.

A thesis statement can simply be a sentence that presents the central topic of the paper. Starting with this basic statement results in a straightforward essay that summarizes aspects of the subject matter. A more effective thesis statement reflects a specific viewpoint or opinion about the subject matter; the essay, in turn, represents the detailed argument that supports this viewpoint. Most teachers prefer this kind of essay; they are interested in your own perspective, rather than a summary of factual information. The more original the thesis statement, the more original—and impressive—your essay will be.

Here are some sample topics:

o American literature of the 1920s
o Modern psychological theories and treatments
o The Cold War

Here are some sample thesis statements that might emerge from the sample topics:

o Most American literature of the 1920s depicts a growing anxiety regarding the dehumanizing effects of industrialization.
o Although dreams play a central role in both Freudian and Jungian theory, there are crucial differences in the ways in which dreams are interpreted.
o The foreign policy of the United States during the Cold War indirectly served to escalate domestic problems on American soil.

Be Specific

An effective thesis statement is not too broad or general; instead, it should say something very specific about your topic. By being very specific, a thesis statement insures that the essay remains focused and does not veer off into unrelated territory that distracts the reader.

Reflect Your Own Ideas

Most professors will be more impressed when you express your own thoughts and ideas rather than regurgitating those of someone else. A more effective thesis statement, therefore, will be original and reflect your own outlook on the subject. Make certain the thesis is phrased entirely in your own words.

Write About a Personal Belief

The body of the essay must make a convincing argument supporting the thesis statement. However, it is extremely difficult to present a solid argument supporting an idea that you don't actually believe is true. Moreover, if the thesis statement reflects a personal belief, the entire essay will bear the strength of your convictions. Don't work against the grain and choose a thesis statement that you don't support.

Choose a Topic on Which You Can Build a Solid Argument to Support

Your goal in writing the essay is to convince your reader that your thesis statement is an accurate one; you want to prove your viewpoint beyond a shadow of a doubt. Therefore, make certain you pick a thesis you know you can prove. When you actually begin conducting research, you may find that you don't necessarily agree with the thesis or that you can't prove it. If this is the case, change the thesis statement.

Write a Single, Direct Sentence

Most essays for academic purposes are limited in length; you probably won't have to write a book-length dissertation. You therefore don't need a long, detailed thesis statement. Make certain you can phrase your thesis statement in one sentence. If you can't do it in one sentence, it indicates you are unfocused and confused about your idea, or that you've chosen a thesis too ambitious to be proven in a single essay.

You may need to fine-tune your thesis statement. Until you've actually begun writing, it is fine to have only a general sense of your thesis. As you conduct research and gain more knowledge of your topic, you'll continue to hone your thesis statement.

Once you have an idea of what your thesis statement will be, it's a good idea to discuss it with your teacher. This will confirm that you are on the right track. Your teacher may also have suggestions on how to conduct research and organize the essay.

Conduct Research

There are essentially two kinds of essays: those that require you to do research from outside sources, and those that do not. Essays that do not require research focus solely on your own thoughts and ideas about a particular topic; those that include research utilize information from outside sources to explain and support your thesis. Your teacher will tell you whether or not you are expected to do research and include other sources in your essay. If the teacher doesn't tell you, then ask.

There are two kinds of sources: primary and secondary. Primary sources are any texts that are the focus of an essay, such as specific works of literature, historical documents, or essays and articles that present certain theories and philosophies. For example, if you are writing about some of Shakespeare's plays, then Romeo and Juliet and Hamlet would be primary sources. If your essay centers on a primary source, you must make certain you read it in detail and take notes on it.

Many essays also incorporate secondary sources. These are books and articles by critics, historians, scholars, and other writers who comment on and address primary sources, as well as other topics and subjects. If your essay involves conducting research, you need to track down secondary sources that address your topic and take notes on them.

Where to Find Possible Sources

There are obviously many sources that address your topic. However, before you read them, you need to find them. Fortunately, there are several resources you can turn to for help in finding possible sources.

The Library Subject Catalog: All libraries list their sources in a catalog, either on index cards or on computer. The entries are usually organized three

ways: by author, title, and subject. If you have a specific source in mind, you can consult either the author or title entries to find out if the library has the source and where it is located. If you are merely looking for general sources, though, you can search according to the subject.

Most libraries organize their subject catalogs according to the standard list of subjects set by the Library of Congress, although some libraries have their own classifications. The library should have a subject list available for you to consult. Sometimes a subject will be divided into subcategories. Try to find whatever subject or subcategory most closely relates to your topic.

WHAT YOU'LL FIND IN THE LIBRARY

Many people think of the library as a kind of big warehouse for books. Although it is true that a library's collection of books can provide you with a wealth of information, most libraries have a great deal more to offer.

The following is a list of holdings a college library is likely to offer:

- Encyclopedias, indexes, dictionaries, bibliographies, almanacs, and other reference guides
- Filmstrips, microfilm, and microform
- Newspapers and magazines
- Academic journals
- Rare document archives
- Videotape and film collections
- Audio recordings
- Slides
- Files of student theses and dissertations
- Maps and atlases

The following is a list of resources and services a college library is likely to offer:

- Typewriter or computer centers (for typing essays, etc.)
- Copy machines or copy services
- Audio/visual screening/listening facilities
- Language labs
- Quiet study lounges and cubicles
- Lockers
- Interlibrary loans
- Search for lost books
- Place holds on books already taken out
- Computers with access to the World Wide Web
- Computerized catalogs and bibliographies
- Librarians

Note: Librarians are the most vital resource in the library; they can provide you with a tremendous amount of help for just about any academic project you pursue. Ask them questions; that's what they're there for.

Any good library should offer some, if not all, of the above resources and services. It's a good idea to take a brief tour of or wander around your library to find out exactly what it offers. Then take advantage of it. If you use the library properly, its resources can make the job of being a student much, much easier.

Published Bibliographies and Indexes: There are many published bibliographies and indexes that list books and other sources, such as academic journals and periodic articles, on a particular subject. These bibliographies compile citations for various books and sources. A citation is a listing for a particular source that includes key information about the book, such as the author, title, publisher, and often a brief summary of the source's content. Bibliographies and indexes are usually located in the reference section of the library. To find a bibliography on your topic, you can either ask the librarian for suggestions or consult the subject catalog.

Lists of Works Cited and Bibliographies in Sources: Most academic books, essays, and journals include their own bibliographies, list of works cited, or suggested further readings. These listings provide sources you might read as part of your research. Each time you read a new book or article, check the author's bibliography or notes to see if there is anything of interest. You can also check the assigned course texts for listings.

Computerized Information Resources: Several indexes, such as the *MLA Bibliography* and the *Reader's Guide to Periodic Literature*, are available via computer. Many libraries have computer monitors set up that enable you to conduct on-line searches. You can instruct the computer to search for sources relating to a particular author, title, or subject, and the computer will put together and print out a listing for you. Libraries have different regulations for conducting on-line searches. Some might require that you meet with a librarian to learn about the system before you use it on your own. You might also have to sign up for time to work on the computer.

The Internet is a valuable tool for finding sources, provided you know how to use it and have access to it. If you have access to the Internet, either at home or at the school's computer center, you can surf the Net to look for sources. Through the Internet, you can gain access to indexes and bibliographies, and also find entire articles from newspapers, magazines, and periodicals. There are now many published guides and books that include simple directions for using the Internet for a variety of purposes, including conducting research.

Keeping Track of Sources

Whenever you find a reference to a source you'd like to investigate, make a note of it. It is extremely important that you write down all relevant information: the author(s), title, publisher (for a book); volume and date (for a periodical or journal); or anthology name and editor (for an essay or article included in another work). This information helps you to find the source and is also necessary when you create your own bibliography.

You can keep this information in a notebook or on a legal pad. However, a particularly efficient way to organize this information is to make bibliography cards. Simply fill out a separate 3 x 5 index card for each source by including all the relevant publication information. The cards provide you with flexibility: You can arrange them in any order, such as alphabetically by author or in order of importance, and you can also group various cards together to make your research more organized. For example, if you are going to a library or bookstore to look for particular sources, you only need to bring those cards that are relevant with you. Finally, the cards provide you with extra room to take brief notes that will help you find the source, such as the call number or general location in the library.

You can also write a brief summary at the bottom of the card that indicates the general focus of the source, as well as some of the relevant topics it addresses. You will encounter a great many sources in the process of conducting research; having these notes can help you distinguish among different sources.

It's a good idea to get in the habit of listing the source on each card in the correct bibliographic format. By doing this, you insure that you have all the required information on the card that you will need for your final bibliography. It can be a real pain to have to go back to the library at the last minute to get information on a particular source.

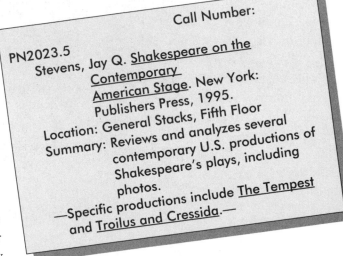

Call Number:

PN2023.5
Stevens, Jay Q. <u>Shakespeare on the Contemporary American Stage</u>. New York: Publishers Press, 1995.
Location: General Stacks, Fifth Floor
Summary: Reviews and analyzes several contemporary U.S. productions of Shakespeare's plays, including photos.
—Specific productions include <u>The Tempest</u> and <u>Troilus and Cressida</u>.—

Jot Down Your Own Ideas

Regardless of whether or not you are required to conduct research, the heart of the essay should be your own ideas. When no outside sources are included, the assumption is made that the entire essay represents your own thinking. However, even when the essay includes other sources, they should only serve to support your ideas.

Jot down your ideas before you actually begin writing the essay. In the course of researching and thinking about your topic, you will develop certain ideas and a sense of the major points you want to make. However, these ideas will probably be mixed together in your head. In order to write a compelling, powerful essay, these ideas need to be organized in a logical manner. You need to get them out on paper, so you can examine them and plan a strategic way to address them in the essay. The writing process is like brainstorming; as you write about one particular idea or point, you'll probably find yourself thinking of many more.

You don't need to worry about things like grammar, spelling, format, or structure when you write down your ideas; you don't even have to write in complete sentences if you don't want to. Just write anything that comes to mind in relation to the topic. You can then refer to these notes—along with any notes from additional sources if this is a research paper—as you organize your essay.

When you are finished jotting down your ideas, read them over and transfer the major ones onto note cards. You can play around with how you organize them in this form, and also integrate them with the note cards from outside sources.

My Idea for Essay

Cycles and Repetitions in LDJ.
There are lots of images that are repeated throughout Long Day's Journey.
— family mealtimes
— cycle of time; one day after another (implied in the title)
— drinking from the bottle then filling with water
— men leaving Mary alone on-stage

Write the First Draft

One of the hardest aspects of writing an essay is getting started. Even after all the research, it can be very intimidating to sit down and start writing. Part of the difficulty comes from the way we tend to view writing. We don't think of writing as a process, and only value the finished product—which is supposed to be flawless. This thinking places tremendous pressure on you; you think the writing needs to be perfect, and often you freeze up with panic, afraid to commit yourself to a single word on paper.

Good writing takes time and effort to produce. You can't expect to get the essay right on the first try, and, in fact, you shouldn't even try. Instead, it's better to write in stages, making changes and improvements with each draft.

Correct grammar and spelling are important parts of an essay because they help make it understandable and readable. However, don't concern yourself with this in your first draft. The most important task is to get all your ideas on paper and to integrate them with notes from other sources. This eliminates a great deal of the stress about writing; you don't have to think about the "rules" at first and can simply concentrate on conveying your ideas.

Start at the beginning of the rough outline and simply start writing. Do your best to explain each of the points. As you need to, refer to your note cards and include quotations or paraphrases from other sources. Make certain you add citations for each sentence that includes information from another source. Keep on writing until you've reached the end of the rough outline. Don't stop to go back or make changes. If you hit a roadblock—a point when you freeze and don't know how to proceed—mark the place with an X and move on to another point. You can go back to the trouble spot later.

This first draft will be extremely rough; the writing will be choppy and difficult to read. But that's okay. It's only the first draft and you are the only one who has to see it. This draft provides you with the raw material for your essay; you can then work on it and refine it until it is a real gem.

Revise and Redraft

Once you have completed the first draft, you should go back to the beginning and read it. Try to read it from an objective standpoint, as if you are someone else reading your work. Because you are so closely tied to your ideas, it will be difficult at first to be objective. Try to think of yourself as an editor going over an article by a reporter. As an editor, it's your job to make certain that everyone will be able to understand the article. You might also try reading it out loud, to listen to how it sounds.

As you read over the draft, ask yourself:

○ Is everything explained fully?
○ Will the reader understand everything as it is currently explained here?
○ Are there any holes or gaps in the argument?
○ Are any ideas underdeveloped or partially explained?
○ Does one idea flow smoothly into the next?
○ What additional information does the reader need to appreciate this point?

Make appropriate notes. Try to anticipate specific questions a reader might have and write them down in the margins.

Now you are ready to go back to the beginning and rewrite. As you rewrite, answer the questions with more information. Revise the essay as many times as necessary, until you are satisfied with it. The essay improves with each draft.

The first few times you read and rewrite, you should focus on the content—the ideas and points that are explained in the essay. Make certain all your ideas are clearly and fully explained and that there are no gaps in the discussion. Examine the organization of the essay and make certain that one point flows smoothly and logically into the next. You might try moving sections of the essay around to see if they work more effectively somewhere else. Check that everything in the essay supports the thesis statement, and take out anything that detracts from the argument.

In later readings, you can concentrate less on the content and more on the writing itself. Pay attention to grammar and to how things are

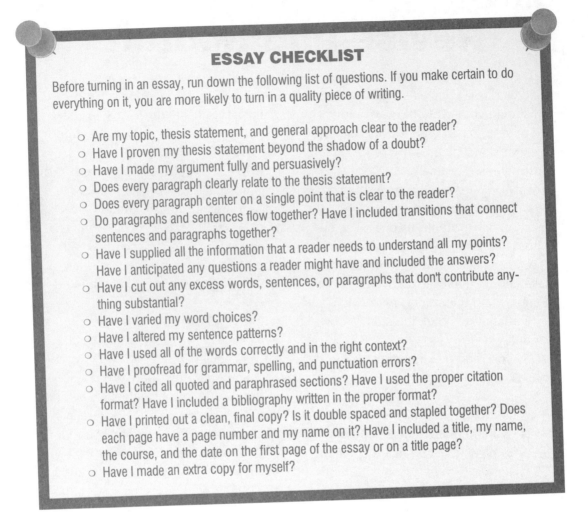

ESSAY CHECKLIST

Before turning in an essay, run down the following list of questions. If you make certain to do everything on it, you are more likely to turn in a quality piece of writing.

- ○ Are my topic, thesis statement, and general approach clear to the reader?
- ○ Have I proven my thesis statement beyond the shadow of a doubt?
- ○ Have I made my argument fully and persuasively?
- ○ Does every paragraph clearly relate to the thesis statement?
- ○ Does every paragraph center on a single point that is clear to the reader?
- ○ Do paragraphs and sentences flow together? Have I included transitions that connect sentences and paragraphs together?
- ○ Have I supplied all the information that a reader needs to understand all my points? Have I anticipated any questions a reader might have and included the answers?
- ○ Have I cut out any excess words, sentences, or paragraphs that don't contribute anything substantial?
- ○ Have I varied my word choices?
- ○ Have I altered my sentence patterns?
- ○ Have I used all of the words correctly and in the right context?
- ○ Have I proofread for grammar, spelling, and punctuation errors?
- ○ Have I cited all quoted and paraphrased sections? Have I used the proper citation format? Have I included a bibliography written in the proper format?
- ○ Have I printed out a clean, final copy? Is it double spaced and stapled together? Does each page have a page number and my name on it? Have I included a title, my name, the course, and the date on the first page of the essay or on a title page?
- ○ Have I made an extra copy for myself?

phrased. Work on individual sentences and paragraphs to insure that they are well written and flow together. Think about ways you might rephrase or reword various sentences to make them clearer or more effective.

When you are finished with your essay, check to make certain you have met the page requirements set by your teacher. Remember, choosing the right topic from the start is the best way to insure your essay will be the appropriate length. However, once you've started writing, you may find your essay is a bit longer or shorter than you intended. If your essay is only half a page or so longer or shorter, most professors will still accept it. However, if it is off by more than half a page, then you need to make adjustments.

If the essay is too long, read through it looking specifically for sentences and paragraphs that don't contribute a significant point to the essay. Examine all the points you've made to support the thesis, pick out whichever one is weakest, and cut out that section of the paper. You can also look for any sections of the paper that needlessly summarize or repeat points that are already quite clear for the reader. Just be certain whenever you make large cuts that you reread the entire essay to see that it still flows smoothly and makes sense.

If the essay is too short, then reread the entire piece looking for any sections that can be developed in more detail. Look for questions a reader might have while reading the essay that you can answer within the text. You also might try to think up additional examples or illustrations you can add to the paper to support major points in more detail. As a last resort, you can look for additional quotations from outside sources you can integrate into the paper as a way of making it longer. Just make certain you discuss the quotations you include; if you just sprinkle them throughout the essay, it will be obvious to the professor that you are merely padding the essay with unnecessary material.

Do a Final Edit

After you have revised the essay several times and are generally satisfied with it, you can edit it. Read the essay slowly and carefully for grammar, punctuation, and spelling errors. Examine each word, sentence, and paragraph. Have resources close at hand, such as a dictionary or grammar handbook, so you can check anything you are not certain about. It's easy to misuse a particular word or to confuse similar words; it's also easy to have a sense of what a word means but have the wrong context for it. You should therefore double-check the definitions of any unfamiliar or complicated words. The same holds true for spelling; if you don't read carefully, you may swear a particular word is spelled correctly when it's actually wrong. Double-check anything you are not 100 percent positive is right.

If you've included quotations and paraphrases from outside sources, you should also double-check the citations. Make certain you've given each source credit and followed the right format.

Turning in an essay that is not carefully edited makes a very poor impression on a teacher. It indicates that you don't take your work all that seriously. Even if the ideas within the essay are good, not taking the time to edit can lower your grade significantly. Make certain you take the time to edit and that you do it carefully.

After you've completed editing this essay, type up or print out the final version. Most teachers (both in high school and college) require that an essay be typed. However, do so even if it is not required. Handwritten essays are difficult for a teacher to read and do not look as professional as typed ones. By typing an essay, you indicate you take your work seriously.

CHAPTER

23

SPEED READING

CRAMMING IT ALL IN

Most people aren't fast readers. The average person can read between 100 and 300 words per minute, and their retention and comprehension level isn't anywhere near perfect. Studies show that people recall only about half of the information that they read. As a college student, you're expected to read thousands of textbook pages per semester. In fact, not only must you read countless textbooks during your college career, it's critical that you remember and understand all of the information that you read.

Wouldn't it be great if you could learn how to read between five and ten times faster, and at the same time improve your comprehension dramatically? Learning to speed read isn't difficult. Anyone with the proper instruction can do it, but it's going to take practice. Just like using any tool, your reading skills have to remain sharp for them to be effective.

When you sign up for a speed reading seminar or purchase a home study speed reading course, if you follow the instructions, you will greatly improve your reading speed and comprehension. You must, however, be willing to invest the necessary time to perfect the skills that you learn. Acquiring the information you need to become a speed reader takes just a few hours, however, you must take what you learn and apply it correctly, by practicing the skills and reading exercises that the various courses teach. Often, this means dedicating between fifteen minutes and one hour per day to practice your newly acquired skills.

You'll realize the benefits of taking a speed reading course almost immediately, however. After all, if you currently spend three hours or more per day reading textbooks or related school materials, wouldn't you love to cut this time down to one hour per day, yet get much more out of the time you spend reading? Speed reading skills are not magic. These courses simply teach you new and innovative ways to take full advantage of your mind's capacity. Learning how to use your eyes correctly when you read and how to focus your mind are skills that are taught by these courses.

For just about every college student, making the financial and time commitment necessary to take a speed reading course is one of the very best investments that can be made.

There are over two dozen different speed reading courses in existence. Just about everyone has heard about Evelyn Wood Reading Dynamics, which is the oldest and probably the most respected speed reading course in the world.

This speed reading system has been around for decades and is absolutely guaranteed to work. Currently, you can sign up for an in-person, six-hour seminar for $149 (which includes a special workbook). These seminars are taught by highly trained, certified instructors who travel around the country offering the course in various cities. Priced at $199, you can also order the complete course on three two-hour videocassettes (which also includes a workbook). As with most speed reading courses, with Evelyn Wood Reading Dynamics, you are taught to see every word on the page, but to read for meaning not words. Speed is increased by reading many words at once, not by reading one of many words. Also, with most of these courses, you will maintain your reading skills as long as you keep using them. Like a sport or musical instrument, if you only play occasionally, your performance will vary widely. Regular use of your reading skills, along with occasional practice to keep them sharp, will give you abilities that will last for a lifetime. Call Evelyn Wood Reading Dynamics at (800) 447-7323 for details on seminars being taught in your city or to order the videocassette course.

In addition to Evelyn Wood, you've probably seen the television infomercials featuring Howard Berg, the world's fastest reader, selling his speed reading course called Mega Speed Reading. In just four hours (plus the additional time needed to practice the Mega Reading methods) you too can become a speed reader. Unlike Evelyn Wood Reading Dynamics, which is taught in-person by trained instructors, Mega Speed Reading is a home study course that comes with a manual, one videocassette, and six audio cassettes. According to a spokesperson for Howard Berg, the emphasis of the $169.95 accelerated learning course is to teach the reader how to focus, improve comprehension, enhance their memory, and build up reading speed using techniques that are different from what Evelyn Wood Reading Dynamics teaches. For information about Mega Speed Reading, call (800) 327-8373. MCI is currently sponsoring a series of lectures by Howard Berg, that are taking place on college campuses around the country and are open to college students.

Ron Cole currently travels to major U.S. corporations and teaches top-level executives a speed reading technique called Super Reading. These executives pay $500 or more to attend one of Ron's seminars. Recently, Ron Cole has taken all of the information he teaches in his seminars and developed a home study course which includes a manual, audio cassettes, self-tests, charts, and all of the necessary information that you need to become a speed reader. The Super Reading home study course currently sells for under $200. Be sure to ask about special student discounts to save up to 50 percent. In addition, for about the same price as the home study course, Super Reading is available on the Internet, using state-of-the-art interactive instruction.

Have you ever finished reading a paragraph and think to yourself "What did I just read? I can hardly remember any of it!"? That's one of the pitfalls of what Ron calls "unorganized reading." Do your eyes ever get tired while you're reading, causing you to feel sleepy? This is another common problem that the Super Reading program, and many other speed reading programs, are designed to help you overcome.

Ron explains that the goal of Super Reading is to allow you to absorb written information, store it, and retrieve it far better and in less time than you do right now. The Super Reading program comes with a money back guarantee if you don't at least triple your reading speed and maintain at least 80 to 90 percent

comprehension. Unlike some other speed reading programs, Super Reading does not train you to skim materials. You will continue to read every word on the page, but you'll learn to view the page and the words on it differently.

"I have been teaching the Super Reading program for over eight years, and I have never refunded anyone's money. Everyone who takes the course and follows our training will dramatically increase their reading speed and comprehension," explains Ron. "Super Reading is based on proven exercises and training that has been around for over thirty years. From all of the research we have done, it doesn't matter if you experience the Super Reading course as a live seminar or if you read our manual and listen to our tapes at home. The benefits are the same. One of the most unique things about our course is that we teach you very specialized eye exercises. Our course also has a very special structure that emphasizes ways to maximize comprehension."

When evaluating any speed reading course, you want to insure that reading comprehension is stressed, because reading material ten times faster, but not remembering what you read is worthless. Likewise, having 100 percent comprehension, but reading at a very slow pace is a waste of time. The best speed reading courses focus first on improving comprehension, and then teach you ways to boost your reading speed. You also want to make sure that the speed reading course you decide to invest your time and money into offers you a way of testing yourself and measuring your progress. Finally, make sure that the course you choose offers a money back guarantee if you don't achieve certain results. "It doesn't matter what other people have done with the course. It only matters what you can do with it," says Ron.

According to Ron, "To master the Super Reading skills, in addition to doing their regular amount of reading, someone has to be willing to practice the eye exercises three times per day, for about ten minutes per session. The people who do the eye exercises on an ongoing basis will see the biggest improvement to their reading speed and comprehension. The course also teaches strategies for reading different types of material. Reading for pleasure, reading a textbook, and reading information on the computer screen while surfing the Internet requires using slightly different skills. Students who take my course go into tests at school knowing that they know the information they're about to be tested on, and that takes a lot of pressure and stress out of the college experience."

To find out more about Super Reading, call (408) 947-6222.

Just like attending college is an investment in your future, so is taking a speed reading course. Ideally, the best time to take one of these courses is during the summer, or during an extended school vacation, so that you can spend the time necessary mastering the speed reading skills. By the time you're ready to start classes again, you'll have the ability to whiz through reading materials much faster, which will lead to higher grades, and less time spent studying.

Throughout your lifetime, you are going to acquire an education as well as specific skills that make you more desirable when you apply for jobs. To set yourself apart from the competition, you want to develop your skills as much as possible. Skills, like being computer literate, knowing how to speak in front of a group of people, and having the ability to read quickly and remember what you read, will come in handy no matter what type of career you ultimately choose.

CHAPTER

RESEARCH ON-LINE

THE NEXT WAVE

Every college and university in America is equipped with a library that contains thousands of books, periodicals, and newspapers that are available to you (whenever the library is open) so that you can do research. In addition, as a college student with a computer, you have access to an incredibly powerful information resource that can make doing research faster and easier than ever before possible—the Internet.

The Internet and the major on-line services (America On-line, CompuServe, and the Microsoft Network) allow you to access timely information on virtually any topic that's stored in computers around the world. This information is available to you, via computer, twenty-four hours per day, seven days per week.

To access the information that's on-line, you either need direct access to the Internet, or a membership to one of the major on-line services. Most colleges provide their students with unlimited free access to the Internet. To gain access to one of the on-line services, such as America On-line, you'll have to sign up and pay a monthly fee. Of course, you're going to need a computer that's equipped with a modem and communi-

cations software in order to get yourself on-line.

If you're connecting to the Internet, your school probably has special software available that provides you with access to the Internet through your school's computer system. If not, you must contact a local Internet service provider in your city, and obtain a copy of an Internet browser software package, such as Netscape Navigator 2.0 or Microsoft Explorer 3.0, that allows you to explore the Internet with ease. All of the major on-line services will provide you with the necessary software, free of charge, for accessing their services. For information on how to get on-line, visit your school's computer center or drop into a local computer store in your city.

Once you're on-line, you have access to information on almost any topic you can imagine, and it's all just a few keystrokes away. Almost every major magazine and many newspapers now have an on-line presence, which means you can search through dozens of back issues based on a keyword or topic in a matter of minutes. This chapter will provide you with a brief introduction on how to find the information you're looking for on the

WHAT IS THE INTERNET?

The Internet is a network of thousands (perhaps millions) of computers around the world that are linked together over the phone lines in order to share resources and information. The computers that make up the Internet are owned by schools, businesses, governments, companies, and individuals. Over the years, the Internet has become so big and complex that very few people actually understand how it works. Luckily, it's not necessary to understand how the Internet works in order to actually use it.

Virtually every college and university in America is linked to the Internet, which means that as a student, you'll have access to it. The most popular part of the Internet is the World Wide Web. The Web allows people to surf sites that contain text, graphics, video, and sound. Sending and receiving e-mail (electronic messages), downloading or transferring software programs, and providing computer users with access to Internet Newsgroups (non-real-time, on-line discussions), are also popular uses of the Information Superhighway—the Internet.

If you're not already familiar with how to "surf the Web," you should definitely sign up for an introductory class at your school or at a local computer store, because knowing how to locate information on the Internet will prove invaluable when it comes time to do research for school. The Internet contains information on virtually every topic you can think of. To search for information by using an Internet search engine, you simply type in a few keywords and you are instantly connected to a Web site or Newsgroup that contains what you're looking for.

The Internet and the World Wide Web are changing constantly as faster modems are developed that allow more complex information to be transferred between computers over standard telephone lines. You can already shop, send and receive e-mail, do research, download software, listen to audio broadcasts, and do all sorts of other cool things on-line, and new uses for the Internet are being created almost daily.

Knowing how to surf the Net has become a skill that is required in many different noncomputer-related careers; so in addition to being a valuable resource while you're in school, by the time you graduate, being computer literate and knowing how to use the Internet will almost definitely be a job requirement. These days, e-mail has become a very popular form of communication, allowing you to instantly send messages to friends, family, and coworkers using your computer. The popularity of e-mail will continue to grow, so establishing yourself on the Net, with your own e-mail address, is important.

information you're looking for on the Internet's World Wide Web.

Now that you have the ability to surf the Web using your computer, the first place you should visit is a search engine, such as Yahoo! (http://www.yahoo.com). A search engine is a Web site that acts like an electronic telephone book listing thousands of other Web sites that you can access. Search engines cost nothing to access, and allow you to locate information by typing a keyword or phrase into the computer. There are over 100 popular search engines available on the Internet that can help you find whatever information you're looking for. A keyword or phrase can be a person's name, company name, product name, publication name, title, or subject. For example, if you're doing a research paper about virtual reality, you can type the term virtual reality into a search engine, and you will be provided with a listing of Web sites you can visit that contain related information.

As you begin exploring the Web, you'll quickly discover that there's a lot to see, so if you're in a hurry to gather information about a specific topic for a project, stay focused. Otherwise, you could find yourself wandering from site to site getting sidetracked by the cool graphics, sounds, and information that are displayed on your screen. When you have more time, you'll definitely want to surf the Web for fun, and locate stuff that interests you.

Searching for information on the Internet can be fun and easy, but it also takes a certain amount of creativity to locate the information you actually need. Before beginning your search, think about what type of information you're looking for and where it might be found on-line. Are you looking for articles from specific magazines, financial data from a specific company, or data on an entire industry? Knowing exactly what you're looking for will make the information much easier to find. After you have determined what type of information you need, think about the various keywords and terms that best

To become more acquainted with everything that the Internet has to offer (the World Wide Web, Newsgroups, e-mail, etc.), consider taking an introductory course or reading one of the many books available that provide a basic overview of what the Internet is all about and how to use it. Having the ability to access vast amounts of information from the comfort of your dorm room, any time day or night, is much more convenient then spending countless hours in a library sifting through books, magazines, and newspapers.

describe what you're looking for. This will help you narrow down your search and pinpoint the information faster.

In addition to being able to research a topic based on a keyword or phrase, you can also access information by

HOT TIPS FOR THE WORLD WIDE WEB

Here are the on-line addresses for popular Internet search engines:

Yahoo!	http://www.yahoo.com
Alta Vista	http://www.altavista.digital.com
WebCrawler	http://query.webcrawler.com
excite	http://www.excite.com
InfoSeek	http://guide.infoseek.com

Electronic Library http://www.elibrary.com (This site alone gives you instant access to over 1,000 magazines, newspapers, news wire services, maps, photos, books, and television and radio transcripts.)

Here is a list of the major on-line services to contact about rates and membership:

America On-line	(800) 827-6364
CompuServe	(800) 848-8990
The Microsoft Network	(800) 386-5550

clicking on subject headings and sub-headings. The Internet's World Wide Web allows users to access information using "hypertext," which means that you can click on specific words or phrases (that are underlined) and automatically get linked to additional information that's related to that underlined word or phrase. Simply pointing the mouse on topics that are displayed on the screen reduces the need for typing, and thus speeds up the search process dramatically.

The main subject headings available through Yahoo! include:

- Arts (Humanities, Photography, Architecture)
- Business and Economy (Directory, Investments, Classifieds)
- Computers and Internet (Internet, WWW, Software, Multimedia)
- Education (Universities, K-12, Courses)
- Entertainment (TV, Movies, Music, Magazines)
- Government (Politics, Agencies, Law, Military)
- Health (Medicine, Drugs, Diseases, Fitness)
- News (World, Daily, Current Events)

○ Recreation and Sports (Olympics, Sports, Games, Travel, Autos)
○ Reference (Libraries, Dictionaries, Phone Numbers)
○ Regional (Countries, Regions, U.S. States)
○ Science (CS, Biology, Astronomy, Engineering)
○ Social Science (Anthropology, Sociology, Economics)
○ Society and Culture (People, Environment, Religion)

Clicking the mouse on any one of these main headings or subheadings will cause additional subheadings to be displayed. This allows you to narrow down your search and ultimately locate specific information.

Once you find a site on the World Wide Web that is of interest, use the Bookmark or Favorites feature of your browser software to store the address of that site. Most sites on the Web have an address that starts with *http://www.(name of site).com.*

Just like a using an ATM or telephone calling card, access to the Internet (or an on-line service) requires that you use a personal password and username. Although your username (e-mail address) is what others will use to send you e-mail, never give your password to anyone.

CHAPTER

25

TAKING TESTS

BRING HOME THE A's

If you've been following the strategies outlined in earlier chapters for taking notes on lectures and reading assignments, then, believe it or not, you've already completed the bulk of your studying. By following those strategies, you've been working with and thinking about concepts relevant to the course all semester; you've gained a comfortable familiarity with the subject and have made it an integrated part of your general knowledge. You could probably go into an exam right now and pass it. However, if you don't prepare for an examination the right way or have the wrong attitude, you are in for some trouble.

You may think that passing an examination is solely a matter of how much of the course material you've got memorized. However, an exam is just as much a test of mental and physical endurance as it is of your knowledge of a particular subject. In that sense, it's somewhat akin to running a marathon. Even though most marathon runners practice every day, they move their training into high gear during the weeks before a major race, running longer hours and further distances so they will be ready for the upcoming event.

You, too, should move your studying into high gear before a test, focusing your energy more on the subject matter. The methods and strategies outlined here will help you do that. You probably won't be surprised to find that, as with the strategies earlier in the book, the key here is to make the study process active. Many students think studying means reading their notes over and over again. There's no guarantee, though, that the more times you read something, the better you'll answer questions about it. You don't need to be a bookworm or genius to ace a test, but you do need to be a "chariot of fire," willing to train hard with the goal of capturing a winning grade on an upcoming exam.

Know What You're in For

One of the things that causes panic in any situation is fear of the unknown. If you don't know what's lurking behind a door, you might very well be afraid to open it, especially when your imagination goes to work and transforms whatever is behind that door into an ax-wielding maniac. Your imagination can also convince you that an upcoming exam will include killer-questions impossible to answer. You can put your mind at ease, though, by finding out as much as possible about an exam *before* you go into the examination room.

In addition to alleviating panic, knowing something about the format of an exam can help you plan your study schedule more efficiently. There are different ways to study for different types of examination questions. If you have an idea of the kinds of questions likely to be asked, you can tailor your study schedule to prepare specifically for those questions.

The following sections suggest ways to find out about an upcoming exam.

Talk to the Professor

The most obvious source for information about an exam is the professor; after all, the professor is the one who makes up the questions. Most professors will take a few minutes during a class to explain the format and the material to be covered. If an exam is approaching and the professor has not made such an announcement, you can take the initiative and ask.

Although you can ask in class, talking to the professor after class or during office hours is, in some ways, more effective. The professor will be more inclined to talk with you at length when it's not taking up other students' time. You'll therefore be able to ask more questions, and, if you're lucky, the professor might offer you more detailed information about the exam than he did in class.

These are some basic questions you can ask a professor about an upcoming exam:

- What will be the format of the exam? Will there be short answer questions? What type? Multiple-choice questions? Essays? A combination of these?

○ How many sections will there be on the exam? How many points will each section be worth?

○ How much of your overall grade does the exam count for?

○ What material from class will be covered on the exam?

○ If the exam is a final, will the exam be cumulative (meaning it covers the entire semester's worth of material)? Or will it only cover a portion of the course material?

○ Does the professor have any suggestions on how to study for the exam?

Try to see the professor at least one week before a scheduled exam; that gives you enough time to plan your study schedule accordingly. However, there's no reason why you can't ask about an exam much earlier in the semester. Although the professor may not have made up the exam yet, she probably has an idea of what the overall format will be and the material it will cover. If you get this information, you can keep it in mind and be on the lookout for possible exam questions as you take notes from classroom lectures and readings.

Try to Find Exams on the Same (or Similar) Courses

You can get a highly accurate sense of what an upcoming exam will be like by looking at previous exams. In addition to providing examples of the kinds of questions likely to be included, these can be used for practice runs to test yourself on the course material.

Some departments keep exams on file so that students can use them as a study resource. You can also try to find someone who has already taken the course and held onto the exams, and who is willing to lend them to you. Just make certain that you are not doing anything unethical in looking at old examinations. If the professor has given a graded exam back to the students, then she knows it is available for anyone to examine. However, if the professor collects the exams and does not return them, then she doesn't intend for them to be distributed among students. If you somehow get a pirated copy of an exam, you are committing a serious breach of ethics that can get you in big trouble. When you consider the penalties, you'll realize that it's just not worth the risk; there are plenty of other study resources you can use.

Ideally you want to find an old exam for the same course you are taking that was made up by your professor. This provides you with the most accurate picture of the exam you can expect to take. If you can't find an old exam written by your professor, you can try to track down exams for the same course given by other professors. Although these exams might not include the exact questions your teacher will ask, they provide a general sense of the questions frequently asked. It is also easier to find old exams when you don't limit your search to your own professor. For example, you can borrow exams from friends at other schools who have taken the same course.

You can also learn a great deal by looking at exams your own professor has given for *other* courses. Although you may not get any clues about the exact questions likely to appear on your upcoming exam, you will get a sense of the kinds of questions your professor asks and their overall level of difficulty.

Listen for Clues

Throughout the semester, keep your ears open for any clues about what might be on an exam. Clues can crop up anytime, so be on the lookout. A professor might say, in a completely casual manner, that a particular concept or term is likely to show up on the exam. After making a certain point, a teacher might say something like, "If I were to ask a question on an exam about this topic, I'd ask you . . ." Anytime your professor makes any reference to an exam, even in an offhand manner, make certain you note and star it.

In addition to blatant clues, the professor will probably give you subtle ones. Exam questions always reflect the professor's personal interests and biases. Even if the course is a basic survey course, there are certain to be some topics your teacher feels are more important for you to know and are therefore more likely to show up on an exam. Anything your professor seems particularly serious or passionate about is a likely candidate for inclusion. Any point your professor makes repeatedly, or gives special attention to, is also more likely to appear on an exam. Star these points in your notes to remind yourself to study them before an exam.

Preparing for Exams: A Step-By-Step Strategy

1. Read over all notes from class lectures and reading assignments.
2. Create master lists from notes.
3. Work with the master lists and quiz yourself.
4. Get help from other sources.

Read Over All Notes from Class Lectures and Reading Assignments

Many students begin to panic before an exam because they've left themselves way too much to worry about at the last minute. An examination approaches, and they find they still have to read assignments they never got to, reread assignments they don't remember, scrounge up notes for lectures they missed, and figure out what their own notes mean if they've forgotten. However, if you have been following the methods outlined in earlier chapters, you should already have clear, comprehensive notes from classroom lectures and reading assignments that include just about everything you need to know for an exam.

To begin studying for an upcoming exam, gather together all your notes from the course in one binder. This should not be a problem, since you've been putting your notes in a binder throughout the semester. Just make certain you now have them all in one place, in a logical order.

The first step is to read these notes from start to finish. It is extremely important that you do this in one sitting, *without interruption*. This will help you concentrate more intently on the material. More important it will enable you to develop a clear picture in your mind of the course material as a whole. Rather than studying various bits and pieces of information related to the subject, you'll now be able to see how everything fits together as part of the overall course.

For each examination, set aside several hours to read through your notes from beginning to end. However, don't study several subjects at once or one subject right after another. If you study several courses within a short period of time, the material can easily become mixed up in your mind, making it more difficult for you to remember specific details. Make certain you take a break of at least two hours before sitting down to read notes from another course.

Create Master Lists from Notes

As you read over your notes, condense and reorganize the material onto three single sheets of paper—the three master lists. The preparation of these lists is itself a part of the study process; by reorganizing the material, you gain a firmer grasp on the course. At the same time, the master lists serve as study tools; rather than having to read through all your notes again, you only need to study these three sheets. Each master list prepares you for a specific kind of examination question.

The Master List of Key Terms: Create a master list of key terms from your notes by writing down any names, dates, concepts, or ideas that are central to the course; do not add any definition or explanation of them. Try to squeeze all the key terms on a single sheet of paper. Don't write down any of them more than once; even if one comes up repeatedly throughout the course, you only need to write it down once. You may also decide to eliminate some key terms from the master list because you

realize, in retrospect, that they aren't all that important.

The Master List of General Themes: Create a master list of general themes. As with the master list of key terms, try to squeeze all the general themes onto a single sheet of paper. If a particular theme recurs throughout the course, you don't need to write it down more than once; however, you should put a star beside it to indicate its importance.

The Master List of Related Concepts: Creating this particular master list is a bit more complicated and will likely take more thought and effort than the other two. However, it will prove helpful in preparing for examination questions of all kinds.

As you read through your notes, try to identify groups of concepts that relate closely to one another. If you've identified such a group, write it down on the master list of related concepts and give it a subject heading.

A common category of related concepts is a principle or idea and the various examples that illustrate or support it. For example, you might be taking a history course in which the professor has argued repeatedly that the latter half of the Middle Ages was marked by an increased pessimism and despair. You might then group together the various events your professor described that indicate this trend:

Reasons for Increased Pessimism in the Fourteenth and Fifteenth Centuries

- Weak kings (Edward II, Richard II) whose power was threatened by the barons
- The One Hundred Years' War
- The Black Plague (1348)
- Skepticism in the church (after the sale of pardons is sanctioned)

Here are some examples of items that you might include on your master list:

- Events and causes (that lead up to them)
- Rules and exceptions
- Similar ideas, concepts, theories, and examples
- Opposite or dissimilar ideas, concepts, theories, and examples
- Chronologies/datelines
- Causes and effects

Try to identify and write down as many of these groups as you can. However, there are any number of ways to organize ideas and you won't be able to identify each and every one. The process of reorganizing your notes this way encourages you to think, using the same kind of logic behind most examination questions.

You might have trouble, at first, fitting all the groups you identify on a single sheet of paper. If this is the case, use more than one sheet. As you work more with the master list, you can make decisions about what to eliminate and eventually condense the list onto a single sheet.

Work with the Master Lists and Quiz Yourself

After your initial reading of all your notes, you should have created three separate master lists—key terms, general themes, and related concepts. The bulk of your preparation for the exam will center on working with these master lists. Each one includes information that will help answer a particular type of question.

Working with the List of Key Terms:
Many short-answer questions, such as multiple-choice, fill-in-the-blank, and true or false questions, are specifically designed to test your factual knowledge, to see if you know about something of significance or the meaning of a particular term. You can't figure out the answer to these questions using reasoning or other kinds of skills—either you know the answer or you don't.

The following sample questions test factual knowledge of key terms:

1. An elegy is
A. a poetic inscription that ends with a witty turn of thought
B. a fourteen-line poem written in iambic pentameter
C. a formal poetic lament after the death of a particular person
D. a long narrative poem documenting heroic actions

2. A fourteen-line poem written in iambic pentameter is
A. a sonnet
B. an epigram
C. an epic
D. an elegy

3. A(n)_____ is a long narrative poem documenting heroic actions.

Although short-answer questions might test you on factual knowledge, you'll also need to know these facts to write essays. As we'll soon see, your primary goal in answering an essay question is to demonstrate to the professor your knowledge and mastery of the subject matter. Therefore, the more key terms you weave into an essay answer, the more you will impress the teacher with your knowledge.

For this reason, becoming very familiar with the key terms is a crucial part of preparing for an examination. For some terms, you will need to provide definitions; for others, you will need to know something that is relevant to the course. This is particularly the case with names of people, places, characters, and dates. For example, on a psychology exam, you might need to define the term *id*. However, you might also need to know significant facts *about* Freud, such as that he conceived of the model of human personality consisting of the id, ego, and superego.

Therefore, as part of your exam preparation, you should spend a certain amount of time learning and testing yourself on the key terms. After you have completed your master list, quiz yourself on the terms. Go down the list and try to define or say something significant about each term on the list. If possible, quiz yourself in private and discuss each term out loud, as if you were explaining it to someone else in the room. This procedure insures that you explain each term fully. Many times, you look at a term, think you know it, and skip to the next one. However, you may not really be able to define the term as easily or as clearly as you think. By talking about each term, you see exactly how much you do or don't know about it. You also begin to feel more comfortable discussing these terms at length, which can help when you write an essay response.

Get Help from Other Sources

In the previous chapters on taking notes and reading texts, we saw that you can always turn to other sources for additional information or to get help if

you are having trouble. Even if you have begun studying for an exam, it's still not too late to get help.

See the Professor: Many students become confused or generally anxious when they first sit down to study for a major exam. In need of advice, they turn to the most accessible and most reliable source of information—the professor. However, if you wait to see a professor a few days before an exam and say, "I'm confused. I really need help. What do I do?," it's really too late in the game. However, if you come with a specific question, you can get specific information. On the other hand, if, as you are studying, you come across something that really confuses you, write down a specific question about it. Bring the question to the professor. In addition to providing you with information about your question, the professor might also offer additional hints about the upcoming exam.

It is also important that you don't rely on the professor as your sole source of help. Once the semester is over, many professors become scarce, which makes it difficult to see them. If you wait to begin studying until after the course has ended, you may not get an opportunity to see the professor. Even if he schedules office hours before an exam, there's no guarantee you'll get to see him—after all, many other students probably have the same idea. Try your best, if necessary, to track down the professor. If you can't, there are other ways to get help.

Reading Other Sources: An important component in the study strategies outlined in previous chapters was reading additional source materials, particularly when you had trouble understanding something from a lecture or reading assignment. If you have enough time, you can still read other sources when you are preparing for an exam. As you go over your notes and prepare the master lists, you may come across terms or ideas that you still don't understand. You also may find that, as time passes, you forget important information. You can turn to other sources or go to the library for more information.

There are many academic encyclopedias and dictionaries, for example, that include listings for the key terms you've studied in class. By consulting these sources, you can find clear and concise explanations of these points. Go to the reference section of the library and ask the librarian to suggest sources.

Even if you are not confused about a particular point, it's a good idea to read some additional sources anyway.

The more sources you read about a particular subject, the more information you receive. And by reading about a subject in depth just before an exam, you immerse yourself in the material; you then enter the examination focused on, and comfortable with, that subject.

Consulting introductions to different editions of important primary texts can provide additional information. For example, an introduction to a particular work of literature will often summarize the plot, describe the characters, and discuss major thematic and critical issues. Reading these introductions helps you recall the work in more detail while providing ideas you might not have considered. You can also look for anthologies and collections that include articles and essays on a particular subject or by a certain writer. For example, an introduction to a volume of *Freud's Collected Writings* might summarize his major innovations, as well as the controversies surrounding them.

Reading about the same topic in several sources is a worthwhile exercise because it shows how the subject can be described in different ways. This is important because examination questions will often be worded in a manner different from the way the material was originally described to you.

Other sources can also provide a variety of examples and illustrations of major principles. Finding additional examples can be particularly helpful in preparing for math and science examinations for which you are asked to complete various problems using different formulas. Seeing a variety of sample problems before an exam makes you better prepared to answer problems yourself; you are able to see the many different problems that relate to a particular formula or principle. You can even find sources with sample problems and solutions, so that you can practice with actual questions.

For all these reasons, consulting with and reading additional sources is a valuable study technique in the days prior to an examination. Your priority, however, is creating and working with the three master lists. Read other sources only if you have additional time during your study preparation period.

Working with Study Partners or Study Groups: In preparing for an examination, many students work with a partner or form a study group. This means of studying is not for everyone, however. Before deciding whether or not a study group would help you, consider these advantages:

○ When you get together with other students, you have the opportunity to learn from one another. One student, for example, may have better notes or a better grasp of a particular subject than you do. You can use the other students as a source of information to flesh out certain points in your own notes.

○ Answering questions from your fellow students will also help you study. Talking about a particular topic is an excellent way to gain familiarity with the material. In the process of describing and explaining a concept to someone else, you come to a better understanding of it yourself.

○ Being part of a study group ensures that you study a certain amount of time before an exam; the group keeps you on a set study schedule. If you have difficulty motivating yourself to study, being part of a study group can give you the jump start you need.

○ Perhaps most important, being part of a study group provides emotional support during a difficult time. Studying for and taking exams is an extremely stressful, emotionally draining experience, especially if you feel alone. Meeting regularly with friends going through the same experience can make you feel better. These meetings alleviate tension as you laugh with your friends and help one another through the rough spots.

In addition, consider these disadvantages:

o If the students in your study group have poor notes and don't really understand the subject matter themselves, you might spend all your time helping them and not receive any help in return. You need to watch out for "study moochers" who haven't done any work all year and merely want to copy your notes.

o Panicky students are also a serious problem in a study group. There may be members who are so stressed out that, instead of providing emotional support, they make you more nervous about an exam than you were before. Additionally, the bulk of the study group's time may be spent trying to calm this one person down or

REVIEW SESSIONS

Prior to an examination, professors occasionally organize formal review sessions in which the professor or a teaching assistant is available to answer questions regarding course material. You should attend these study sessions, even if you don't have a question. You never know what hints a professor might give about what will be on the test. It's also helpful to hear the professor or assistant describe again the major concepts and key terms. Try to use some of their phrases and terminology in your essay responses.

Be aware, though, that these sessions tend to attract panicky students who use the time to voice their own fears and anxieties about the exam. In addition to wasting time in the session, these students can also make you feel stressed out. Do your best to ignore them. The only person you need to listen to at the review session is the professor or teaching assistant. Another problem which might arise is that one or two students will dominate the entire session with their questions. If you have a question, ask it right at the beginning to guarantee you'll be heard.

discussing only those concepts he or she doesn't understand.

o Study groups often don't use time efficiently. You may spend several hours with a study group and find you've only covered a small portion of the material, much less than you could have studied on your own. There are several reasons why this might occur. Whenever a group of students get together, there is going to be a certain amount of chatting, joking, and socializing taking place. Another problem is that a large portion of time might be spent discussing some point you already understand; that time might be better spent studying something you still don't understand.

The way to avoid some of these major disadvantages is by choosing the right people to work with. A good study group involves give and take among all members; all should be willing to work and should have something valuable to contribute to the group. It's also a good idea to limit the size of the group; any more than five members will probably waste more time and be more trouble than it's worth.

At the same time, if you feel you work better on your own, don't feel you are at a disadvantage. Being in a study group is no guarantee of study success.

On Exam Day

The most crucial thing to remember on the day of the exam is to set your alarm and give yourself enough time to get ready, especially if your exam is in the morning. More than one student has slept through a major exam, and it's hard to get sympathy from the professor when this happens. If your alarm is unreliable, or if you have the habit of turning it off in your sleep or hitting the snooze button, then set several alarms.

You may even want to have a friend or relative give you a wake-up call.

When you take a shower that morning, try talking out loud about some of the key terms or general themes you've prepared on the master list. This mental exercise serves to get your brain warmed up and focused on the subject matter. (Since you are in the shower, you won't feel awkward talking out loud.)

STUDY SCHEDULE AND CHECKLIST

Before you begin studying for the exam (before classes end):
o Get information from the professor on exam content and format.
o Try to get sample tests.
o Find out the date, time, and location of the exam.
o Consider joining a study group with other hardworking and intelligent students.

Five to seven days prior to the exam:
o Read through all your notes from classroom lectures and reading assignments.
o Create the three master lists (key terms, general themes, and related concepts). Take four to six hours per subject to do this.

Two to five days prior to the exam:
o Quiz yourself on each master list for each subject every day.
o Work with cue cards and use other memorization techniques to learn key terms.
o Take notes on general themes and talk your way through possible essays.
o See the professor to ask last-minute questions, if you have them.
o Meet with study group or partners, if you opt to do this.
o Read other sources, if time allows.
o Make certain you know where to go for the exam. Confirm the day, time, and location. If you are unfamiliar with the test site, go there before the test day so you can see exactly where it is and how much time it takes to get there.

The night before the exam:
o Give yourself one final read-through of the master lists.
o Talk your way through possible essays.
o Make a cram sheet of terms you still can't get down.
o Relax: See a movie or watch TV.
o Get together stuff to bring to the exam: pens (that work), a watch (that works), candy, gum, a drink, your final cram sheet, and other materials you may need (such as a calculator, books, etc.).
o Get a good night's sleep.
o SET YOUR ALARM BEFORE GOING TO SLEEP!

The day of the exam:
o Talk about some key terms and general themes in the shower for a mental warm-up.
o Eat a meal high in carbohydrates.
o If you have an afternoon or evening exam, use the morning for a final read-through of your master lists.
o Make certain you bring writing utensils and a watch to the exam.
o Get to the exam early to choose a good seat.

If your exam is in the afternoon or evening, you can read over your master lists in the morning. But don't over-burden yourself. A final read-through should be all you need to get in the right frame of mind for the exam. Don't spend this time trying to memorize or learn new material. After this read-through, do something to take your mind off the exam, such as taking a walk or watching TV.

On the day of the test, eat a high carbohydrate meal; carbohydrates, as many athletes know, give your body an energy boost. (A great meal to have before an exam is macaroni and cheese, because you get a mix of carbohydrates and protein.) Don't eat a large meal, though—that will make you sleepy.

Make certain you know exactly where the exam is being given and leave yourself enough time to get there. Try to get to an exam about fifteen minutes before it is scheduled to start; this will ensure you don't arrive late, flustered, and out of breath. You also want to have the benefit of the entire allotted time, from the first minute to the last.

Bring several pens of blue or black ink, or pencils and a sharpener if it is a standardized test, and a good watch. You might also want to bring some gum, candy, or a drink, if it is allowed. Make certain your watch is working or that there is a clock in the room: It is crucial to keep track of time during the exam.

When you get to the exam, choose your seat carefully. You might, for example, want to sit near a window so that you can look up every so often and take a break. Also, you might want to sit where you can see the clock.

Before the exam begins, avoid talking about anything related to the test with other students, especially alarmists and panickers. You can sit at your desk and glance over your master lists or a last-minute cram sheet if you've made one. But don't get involved in a detailed question and answer session with other students; it's really too late to learn any major point. Moreover, if you listen to someone else, you risk becoming confused about material you were previously quite confident about. This will only serve to make you more anxious. Stay calm so you can take the exam with a clear head.

REWARDS AS MOTIVATION

You're not going to want to study every time you should. Nevertheless, you're going to have to motivate yourself somehow to do work even when you don't feel like it. One way to do this is to reward yourself when you accomplish specific study tasks.

The time remaining after you've completed your study tasks for a particular day is your personal free time. This in itself should serve as a reward to get you motivated to work. For example, if you want to watch television at night, you can force yourself to work efficiently during the day. Similarly, if you want to go to a party on the weekend, you can try to get all your work done during the week. You just need to remind yourself of the fun activities waiting for you when you finish working.

However, even with the promise of free time as a reward, you may still find it difficult to get motivated and begin working. You can provide yourself with additional rewards as you study. Set small goals, and reward yourself each time you fulfill them. For example, if you have several hours blocked off on Tuesday night for reading forty pages, promise yourself a snack after you've gotten halfway through the assignment. This will at least get you started.

These rewards don't need to be extravagant. A reward can simply be a short break to do something you like getting ice cream, talking on the phone, going for a walk, listening to music, or whatever. Just make certain the "reward" time is a short break lasting no more than twenty to thirty minutes.

This rewards system is particularly helpful if you have to spend long hours at work, such as when studying for an exam or writing a paper. If you think of yourself as slaving away for many long hours, it will be extremely difficult to motivate yourself to begin work. However, if you divide the task into several smaller ones and promise yourself a small reward at the completion of each one, it will be much easier to get started. You know then that when you sit down to work, a reward of some kind is not all that far away.

When you finish a major task, such as completing an essay or taking a final exam, it's nice to give yourself a bigger reward—a new CD or a fun evening out. These rewards can help you get through the especially difficult work periods during the school year.

Finding a Comfortable Study Space

Many people seem to think that the only way to study is at a bare desk, with a hard-backed chair, in some minuscule study cubicle in the library. Although this setting does wipe out any outside distraction, it's such a gloomy, sterile atmosphere that it turns studying into a form of medieval torture. Studying just doesn't have to be that depressing.

Since you'll spend long hours at the books, reading over your notes and assigned texts, you may as well make yourself comfortable. If you work in a space where you're relaxed and feel at home, you'll study more often and more effectively. Study anywhere you feel comfortable—in your room, in bed, at the library, in an empty classroom, at a café, outside, in the park—provided that you do two things: Minimize outside distractions, and promise yourself to make a change if you don't get the work done.

In choosing a place, consider the amount of outside distraction—such as friends stopping by, the phone ringing, and loud music—and do what you can to minimize it. Even the library may not be free of distraction; if everyone you know goes there to study, you may

spend more time chatting with friends than studying. You can, though, minimize the distraction by avoiding the main study lounge and finding a quieter section of the library, where you won't run into many people you know.

There's nothing wrong with studying in your room so long as you get work done. Your room is, after all, the space where you are most at home. However, you will need to minimize distractions there as well. If you are frequently interrupted by the phone, turn the ringer off; if friends frequently disturb you, keep the door closed.

If you decide to study in your room, it's a good idea to designate a spot as your main work space. Your desk is probably the best place. However, your room need not have a sterile, austere atmosphere. Since it's your room, you can personalize it by hanging up posters or photographs.

You can even listen to music while you study, just as long as it doesn't distract you. Listening to something old that you are very familiar with will distract you less than something brand new. If you study outside your room, you can try bringing a walkabout tape or CD player along and listening to relaxing music. That's one way to make wherever you study feel a little more like home.

Whatever study space you choose, try to do most of your work there. This will help make studying more of a habit. Arriving at that space—whether it's your desk in your room or your favorite spot in the library—alerts you to the fact that it is time to work. You can begin work more easily in a familiar setting than you can in a strange environment.

You can also designate different places for different study tasks. For example, you might decide to read assignments for class at home, but go over lecture notes in the library. Studying in a variety of locations does make the process less tedious. However, you should make it a habit to do the same study tasks in the same place so they will seem more routine.

Sometimes, for whatever reason, you'll find it difficult to pay attention. When this happens, a simple change of scene may be all you need to refocus on your work. If you've been studying at your desk, go out somewhere, to a coffee shop or the library, and see if you get more done. However, if you find you consistently don't get a great deal of work done, make a more permanent change. If, for example, you are so

relaxed studying in your room that you always fall asleep, then that's probably not the best place for you to work.

Remember, pick a work space where you feel relaxed and comfortable, but one where you also get work done. This means being honest with yourself. Only you know whether you are studying effectively; if you aren't, then you need to initiate changes.

No Time to Nap: Staying Awake While You Study

It might sound like a joke, but falling asleep while reading or studying is a problem that plagues many students. The need to sleep is powerful—and to fight it, you need to take equally strong measures. Here are a few important suggestions:

○ Get enough sleep at night. There's a simple reason why so many students fall asleep while studying, and it's not necessarily boredom. They're just tired. Of course, it's difficult when you are a student to get a good night's sleep all the time, and you shouldn't expect to. However, don't make a habit of staying up late all the time. Try as often as possible to get six to eight hours of sleep a night.

○ Don't get too much sleep. You might not realize it, but there is such a thing as *too much sleep*. For most people, six to eight hours of sleep a night is sufficient. If you get more sleep than your body needs, you can feel sleepy all day long.

○ Exercise regularly. If you exercise regularly, you'll sleep better at night and be more energized during the day. That means you'll be more focused on your classes and your studies.

○ Become alarmed. If you tend to fall asleep while studying, set an alarm. You can purchase an inexpensive travel clock or wristwatch equipped with an alarm and have it nearby while you study. The alarm should be loud enough to wake you up but quiet enough not to disturb those around you. If possible, set the alarm to go off every fifteen minutes. If you can't set it to go off regularly, set it for a specific time (such as a half hour after you've begun studying), and continue to reset it each time it goes off.

○ Arrange for wake-up calls or visits. If you don't trust an alarm, have a friend check on you every so often. The easiest method is to arrange to study together; that way you can both keep an eye on the other and keep each other awake. Of course, you have to be careful that you both don't fall asleep at the same time, and also that you don't spend too much time chatting. If you are studying in your room, you can have a friend or relative give you a phone call every hour or so to check up on you.

○ Take breathers. If you become too comfortable while studying, it's easy to fall asleep. You should plan to get up and walk around at regular intervals—preferably outside. Even though fresh air can do wonders for waking you up, limit your walks to just five minutes. When you return to studying, you'll feel revived and better able to focus.

○ Stay actively involved. The more engaged in the material you are, the less likely you'll succumb to sleep. Rather than just reading the words on the page, have a conversation with yourself (in your mind) about what you read; read a few lines and then comment on them.

○ Don't get too comfortable. It's important to be comfortable while you study because the more relaxed you are, the more open your mind will be. Additionally, being comfortable makes studying less tedious. However, there is such a thing as being too comfortable. If you find yourself constantly falling asleep, you should change your study habits. For example, if you study on a couch or bed, you might need to sit at a desk, where it is more difficult to fall asleep. If you listen to music, you might need to change your selection to something that will keep you up rather than lull you to sleep. Remember, study in an atmosphere you feel relaxed in, but not so much so that you cannot stay awake.

ON THE SHELF: REFERENCE BOOKS YOU SHOULD OWN

There are certain reference guides that every student should own, and they are well worth the investment. These books prove themselves indispensable at various times, from helping you to write essays and papers to enabling you to look up additional information as you read required texts and your classroom notes.

- A Collegiate Dictionary—This is the most important reference book for a student to own. As you go about your required reading for courses, you'll encounter many new vocabulary words you'll need to know in order to follow what you read. Additionally, as you write essays, you should double-check the spelling and meaning of any words for which you are not 100 percent certain of the correct usage.
- A Thesaurus (preferably in dictionary format)—This is a resource for improving your writing. By looking up synonyms or frequently used words, you can alter your usage with synonyms and antonyms and make your writing much more interesting.
- A Specialized Dictionary—There are many of these dictionaries on the market that list words, names, and terms within specific fields, such as literature, science, philosophy, and mythology. Depending on what areas you study, you may wish to purchase one or several of these guides.
- A World Atlas—You'd be surprised how much information you can get from a good atlas. As you read or write, you can dip into it for various facts, from identifying capitals to basic information about countries. As you come across a place name in your reading, you can enhance your sense of it and of its place in the world by opening your atlas.

Making an Impression

There's no way around the fact that grades are a central part of most schools. A large portion of a grade is based on objective information, such as the number of short-answer questions you got right or wrong or the number of days you attended class. However, grading is also subjective: It is based in large part on the teacher's impression of you. Although this impression can't change the number of exam responses you got right or wrong, it can influence other aspects of your final grade. For example, a final grade will often reflect a grade for class participation, which is much more difficult to measure than the number of right or wrong responses.

It is extremely important that you try to make a good impression. However, you also need to be careful how you do it. If you overdo your effort, it can seem insincere and backfire. For example, if you interrupt the lecture or class discussion simply to make some comment that demonstrates how smart you are, you will not impress the teacher. Moreover, the teacher might resent that you've interrupted class for a nonrelated point in an obvious attempt to gain Brownie points.

The impression you want to convey is not necessarily how smart you are, but that you are a conscientious student who is willing to work hard to learn. There are several specific things you can do to make this impression.

Perfect Attendance

Nothing is more off-putting to a teacher than a student who consistently comes late to class, or doesn't come at all. Coming late not only disrupts the entire class but also indicates to the teacher that you don't care about the class. Even in a large lecture course, where you think you might slip in unnoticed, a teacher can notice a student who arrives late. You should therefore make it a habit to get to class on time. If you have a special reason for being late, make certain you see the professor during office hours to explain the situation and apologize.

Coming late to class is a disruption; not coming at all is a major problem that can seriously affect your grade. In some smaller classes, a teacher will take attendance. If this is the case, you should obviously make certain you attend as often as possible. Having perfect attendance will probably impress the teacher when it comes time to give your class participation grade.

Even if a teacher does not take attendance, it is still worth going to class as often as you can. For one thing, being there on a regular basis insures that you are exposed to all the course material, which in itself will probably improve your grades. Moreover, if you attend class regularly, the teacher will consider you a familiar face.

Office Visits

If a teacher doesn't know you by name, however, it won't matter what image he or she has of you when it comes time to assign your grade. While professors usually know students by name in small classes, it is almost impossible to get to know all of them in large lecture classes. You should therefore make certain to see the professor at least once during office hours to introduce yourself. To help break the ice, try to come up with a specific question to ask about the class. During

the course of your discussion, you can tell the professor a bit about yourself and your academic interests. Doing this insures that the teacher has an impression of you as an individual, not as another face in the crowd.

Class Participation

When class participation is part of the grade, many students make the mistake of thinking that they just need to talk a lot to get a good grade. However, there are many kinds of comments and questions, and some are much more intelligent and impressive than others.

Asking questions indicates a general interest in the class. However, students who constantly raise their hands and ask very basic questions about fairly obvious points can make a bad impression—they appear too lazy to make an effort to understand something for themselves. There is, however, a way to phrase a question that sounds more intelligent. For example, if you simply raise your hand and say, "I really don't get this. What does it all mean?" you sound like you just don't want to make the effort to understand the topic. However, if you say to a professor, "I see the point about Y and Z, but I'm having trouble understanding how they relate to X," you are asking a more specific question that reflects that you have worked to understand something. Try to make your questions very specific to indicate you have some knowledge and a genuine interest in clarifying a point.

Another way students earn credit for class participation is by making comments during class discussions. However, many students who feel compelled to say something in class will say whatever pops into their heads. If the comment restates something that has already been said or merely points out something obvious, it won't impress the teacher; in fact, it can indicate you haven't been paying close attention. If you want to make a general comment, make certain it contributes something meaningful or makes a new point.

Not everyone is comfortable participating in class discussions or asking questions in front of large groups, and this doesn't necessarily detract from the class participation portion of a grade. If you are shy, visit the professor during office hours and discuss the course—this will demonstrate that you have an active interest in the class.

Take Pride in Your Work

Being a conscientious student means you take pride in your work. It indicates you are not just going through the motions of showing up for class, but are taking your work seriously. The quality of the work you turn in indicates how conscientious you are. For example, an essay that has been carefully proofread and neatly typed shows you've put work into it and care about how it appears. However, an essay smudged with Liquid Paper and pencil marks, with spelling errors, and with a coffee stain on the cover page, sends the message that you really don't care all that much about the work. And the teacher will then not care all that much about reading it or the grade you get.

While there are specific things to do that show how conscientious you are, you also need to adopt a conscientious attitude. That way whatever you do, whether you are conscious of doing it to impress the teacher or not, will reflect well on you. Take pride in your work as a student, take your job seriously, and everything you do will reflect this positive attitude.

IMPORTANT POINTS TO REMEMBER

1. Develop productive study habits and make them a part of your daily routine. Change bad habits into good ones.
2. Treat being a student like a job: be professional, serious, and organized.
3. Set tasks for each day, week, and month.
4. Manage your time carefully: create a schedule that gives you flexibility each week to fulfill new tasks.
5. Take control over your education and make the most of it.

 DISABILITIES

CHAPTER

26

EXTRA HELP

LEARNING DISABILITIES WON'T HOLD YOU BACK

Research shows that nearly one out of every ten Americans is born with some form of learning disability, such as dyslexia. Having a learning disability doesn't mean you're stupid, it just means that you have to learn things a bit differently. The way your brain processes information is different from that of other people. Some people with dyslexia have trouble reading and writing because they mix up or transpose letters, for example, *b* and *d*, *l* and *i*, or *p* and *q*. Other people with dyslexia has trouble with math or with memorizing information.

There are many different degrees of severity when it comes to learning disabilities, yet with the proper training and tutoring, people with dyslexia (and other learning disabilities) can learn to compensate. For example, studies have shown that people with dyslexia who have trouble writing can use a personal computer and word processing software (with a spelling checker) to help them overcome their disability. Likewise, people who have trouble reading can take full advantage of books-on-tape programs, and listen to recordings of their textbooks and related reading materials.

Many extremely successful and famous people have had dyslexia or another form of learning disability, yet they have overcome their disability. For those who are learning disabled, college is going to be challenging. Passing courses and earning good grades will require extra work and quite possibly a considerable amount of tutoring. What you should know, however, is that from a legal standpoint, every college or university in America that receives any amount of government money is required to provide students with learning disabilities the extra support they need. A growing number of schools even have special programs to assist students with learning disabilities. If you're willing to work extra hard and keep yourself extremely organized, even if you're severely learning disabled, you will be able to succeed in school and in whatever outside activities you choose to participate in.

As an incoming freshmen who is learning disabled, hopefully, when you applied to the school you will be attending, you were open and honest about your disability. Your immediate task should be to locate the faculty advisor or person at your school who is responsible for assisting learning disabled students. This person will be extremely helpful to you when it comes to arranging tutors and communicating with faculty members about your special needs. You will find, in just about every educational institution, that some faculty members simply know nothing about learning disabilities or they don't believe in them. These are the professors you want to avoid taking classes with, and having a faculty advisor who understands your situation will help you choose the best professors so that you can get the best education possible.

At the start of each semester, make a point to meet with your professors privately and discuss your situation and your special needs. Work out in advance with your professors how you will take exams (orally, on an un-timed basis, etc.). Also, if you'll need to be tutored in a specific subject, work with your professor to find a tutor that can help you throughout the semester.

Although students with learning disabilities each have their own unique college experience, Molly Sullivan has an interesting story that proves that people with learning disabilities can excel. Molly was tested and diagnosed with dyslexia in first grade. Since that time, she has learned how to compen-

sate for her disability by using tutors and by working with learning disability specialists. Sure, Molly always had trouble in school, but she worked extra hard to achieve success. Early in her life, she also discovered that she has a passion and great skill in the sport of fencing. In fact, by the time she was ready to apply to college, she was considered by college admissions offices as a Blue Chip Athlete.

Molly attended the University of Notre Dame. Because of her fencing abilities, she was given a full four-year athletic scholarship. By her graduation year, she qualified and became a member of the United States Olympic Fencing Team and competed in the 1988 Olympics.

"When I was still in high school, I knew my only chance to attend a good college would be if I earned a full scholarship, because my family didn't have a lot of money. Because of my fencing, I had five scholarship offers, however, I also needed a school that would offer special programs to help me deal with my dyslexia and insure me a good education. As I was talking to the various schools, I made it very clear that I was going to need help and special services in order to get through the classes. At Notre Dame, they offered several different tutoring programs that I was able to take advantage of," explains Molly.

"Some of my professors were very willing to modify their teaching style or requirements in order to accommodate my needs, and some weren't. Some professors are more flexible then others, so I relied on the guidance from my advisors regarding which professors to select when signing up for classes. One thing I did to insure that my professors always knew that I was trying my hardest to succeed was to never miss any classes. I also met with the professors when I began having trouble. Once my professors realized that I was really trying, they become a lot more understanding of my situation. A lot of people just don't understand what it's like having a learning disability, because it's not something you can physically see. If I were in a wheelchair, people would see that I had a disability. That's not the case with a learning disability, so at times, it's the student's job to teach the professors about what having a learning disability is all about."

Molly believes that it's not always totally necessary for a student with a learning disability to select a school that has a special program in place to deal with their disability. "It depends on what type of person you are. If you're someone who can speak up for yourself and let it be known exactly what you need in order to get by, then you can probably be successful at almost any school. If you're not too comfortable or assertive about your learning disability, I would definitely recommend that you look into schools that offer organized and well-established programs for learning disabled students. It all has to do with your comfort level with yourself and your disability. It's very easy to fall through the cracks at a college or university, because there are usually a good number of students who need special attention, and you have to be willing to fight for your rights when it becomes necessary to do so."

The key to Molly's success has always been total organization. "Time is an important thing. The more things I had to do, the more organized I had to be. The more organized I was, the more I got done. At first, I tried not to overextend myself, by taking only four classes, instead of five. I then took summer classes to make up the difference. As a learning disabled student, it is important that you never get overwhelmed. I tried to always maintain a routine for myself. My classes were in the mornings, I'd have the afternoon free to study, and then I spent my late afternoons at fencing practice. I'd usually have my evenings free. I tried to develop my schedule so that I had big blocks of time each day during which I could study or work with tutors. I also had a special place to study, outside of my dorm room, where I would not get distracted. When I was studying, I had to stay very focused. If I tried to study in the dorm, I'd wind up hanging out with friends."

Molly suggests that students with learning disabilities make it a point to learn about services that are available to them, both on and

off campus. Organizations such as Recordings for the Blind and Dyslexic make textbooks and other books available on audio cassette. These services are available free of charge.

During Molly's senior year in college, she maintained a full course load, plus her collegiate fencing schedule, her national team schedule, and her international team schedule. "I did this by loading all of my classes on Tuesdays and Thursdays. This gave me Mondays, Wednesdays, Fridays, and weekends off. I always brought my school work along while traveling, and studied on the road. The most important thing for college athletes on scholarships to realize is that their education is a gift. Student athletes sometimes tend to focus more on their sport then on their education, and that's a big mistake. College athletes have to concentrate on getting the

best education possible, because you never know when or if you will be injured and your athletic career will come to a sudden end. Student athletes have a tremendous opportunity to excel in their sport, plus get a good education, and that's something they should take full advantage of and always keep in perspective. It's important not to get caught up in the hype."

Molly's dreams of getting a top-notch education and participating in the Olympics have come true. These days, Molly continues fencing, plus she travels around the country speaking to young people about overcoming their learning disabilities, goal setting, and self-esteem. "What kept me motivated to succeed was that people always told me that I couldn't do things, and I had to prove them wrong. I was told that I wouldn't get into college, and I did. I was told that I would never graduate from a school like Notre Dame and I did. And I was told that I'd never make the Olympic fencing team and I did. To succeed, you have to believe in yourself and your abilities. To achieve anything, you have to set goals for yourself. I use the image of a ladder to help me define my goals. At the top of the ladder is my ultimate goal, and each step on the ladder

is a smaller goal or objective that I must accomplish in order to achieve my ultimate goal. Thus, I break up my ultimate goal into many smaller, more manageable and achievable goals. The ladder itself has to be on a strong foundation, or else it's going to fall, so I begin by setting the groundwork for achieving my ultimate goal, and then I take one step at a time. Trying to skip steps makes the ladder unstable, so you have to take each step in order, and if you do this, it becomes fairly easy to reach your goals and make your dreams come true."

One excellent resource for all dyslexic students is the Orton Dyslexia Society. This national organization has over 10,000 members and local chapters in most major cities. The Orton Dyslexia Society was designed to help people with this learning disability learn about the many services that are available to them. For more information, call (800) ABC-D123 or (410) 296-0232. Recordings for the blind and dyslexic can be reached by calling (609) 520-8014.

CHAPTER

2 7

INTERNSHIPS
PLAN NOW, BENEFIT LATER

aving just gotten into college, one of the last things on your mind is what you want to be when you grow up. Once you graduate, your big challenge in life will be to land your first job, ideally in an occupation that you really enjoy and in which you will be successful. Even though your first big job search is still years away, it's something you should start thinking about now, in order to truly prepare yourself and to give yourself the best possible edge.

Unfortunately, the job market, no matter what industry or career path you choose, is extremely competitive. When you're a senior in college and you begin interviewing for entry level-positions, you'll be competing against many other recent grads for a limited number of entry-level job openings.

So, what's the good news? Well, if you spend your time in college getting the best education possible, and taking a few simple steps toward preparing for your first job search, you'll find yourself in a much better position later on. The ultimate trick will be to set yourself apart from the competition. When you begin going on job interviews, you'll want to prove to the interviewer that you're not only smart, competent, and motivated, but also qualified for the job for which you're applying.

What employees are looking for is proof that you can handle the job. The proof they're looking for is often previous work experience. The trick to getting some practical work experience under your belt is to participate in at least one internship program while you're in school. Companies love interns because they work for free (or for little pay). Interns often get placed in positions at companies where they can learn a lot, meet many successful people, and develop practical skills. In addition, they often receive course credit for participating in the program.

Yes, participating in an internship program will most likely mean giving up your afternoons during the school year, or giving up your winter or summer vacation, but that internship experience will provide practical "real world" training that every employer looks for. Listing this experience on your resume gives you instant credibility. More importantly, many companies actually wind up hiring (or at least offering jobs to) their best interns once they graduate. No matter what industry you choose, if you speak with top-level executives they'll tell you how important it is to participate in an internship program while you're still in school.

An internship is very different from taking a part-time summer job at a mall or local fast food restaurant. Even if your school doesn't offer a formal internship program, as a college junior or senior, you can still approach a company and ask to work for them as an intern.

By the time you reach your junior or senior year in college, you should have a general idea of what your interests are and what type of career you want to pursue when you graduate. As soon as you pinpoint a career, find a company that you'd like to work for, and then apply for an internship at that company. Use your time as an intern to learn about the company and industry. You may discover that you absolutely love the work, in which case, when the internship is over, you'll have valuable work experience and an important addition to your resume. You could, however, discover that you hate the work, in which case the internship also proved to be valuable, because you still have time to change or modify your major in order to pursue other interests.

There are many things that you'll be learning in school as part of your college education. The one thing that no college or university can teach you, however, is what it's like working in the real world. This is something that you have to discover for yourself, and an internship is a wonderful opportunity to begin making that discovery.

It is important to remember that when you ultimately graduate and start looking for a job, the people who interview you are likely to put much more weight on your internship experience than on your school-related activities. For example, an employer at a newspaper would most likely prefer to see listed on your resume an internship at a major daily (or local) newspaper rather than that you wrote for your college newspaper. Ideally, you should do both. Likewise, if you apply for a job at an accounting firm, an internship at an accounting firm would be much more impressive to the employer than summer work at a fast food restaurant.

Tips for Choosing an Internship

1. Think about what type of job or career you're interested in pursuing. Start thinking about it now, and during your freshmen, sophomore, and junior years at college, take courses that cater to those interests.

2. Find a handful of companies in your geographic area that are within the industry that interests you. This will require some research. Since you will be listing this internship on your resume, look for well-known and established companies that are respected. Every industry has magazines and publications to which you can subscribe. By reading these magazines over a several month period, you'll learn who the industry's key players are, who the competition is, and whether or not the industry as a whole is expanding.

3. Think about what division or department of the company you're interested in working for. If you have a strong interest in marketing, for example, then you want an internship working in the marketing department of a company.

4. Contact the company you're interested in, and ask if they offer an established internship program. If so, contact the person at the company who coordinates the internship program. Your school will most likely have many contacts at companies that are looking for interns. If the company does not offer an internship program, contact an executive who works for whatever division within the company that interests you (marketing, advertising, product development, research, accounting, etc.)

5. Be willing to "give 100 percent" to your internship. Do your best work and meet as many people as you can.

6. Start exploring internship opportunities early (at least six months before the actual internship will begin). This will give you the best selection of opportunities, plus allow you to find an internship that caters to your interests. Just

about every successful executive working in the business world knows that to truly be successful, you have to be working in a job that you absolutely love. Think of your internship as a testing ground for helping you to fine-tune your interests and find an industry and a career that you will enjoy and that will offer you long-term growth potential.

7. Even if you're planning on entering into your family's business upon graduation, get your internship experience outside of the company your family owns or manages. Working in the same industry is fine, but if you're working for another company, you'll learn more about the industry as a whole, plus you'll learn how other companies operate. This experience will be beneficial once you begin working for your family business.

You've probably heard stories about how some companies abuse their interns, making them spend countless hours making photocopies, getting the executives coffee, or running to the dry cleaners to pick up an executive's suits. In many cases, that's part of what being

an intern is all about. Before accepting an internship, ask what your responsibilities will include, and make sure that your internship will be a learning experience. Count on the fact that you'll be making lots of copies or getting people coffee, but also make sure that you'll have the opportunity to work with people who can also give you more important

responsibilities and allow you to gain experience.

Once you're involved in an internship, one sure way to get more responsibility involves dedicating some additional free time toward your work. Look specifically for executives and middle managers who are stressed out and overworked. Volunteer to spend some extra time helping one of the people you pinpoint as needing assistance. You'll still have your other internship responsibilities to deal with, but by offering to help out someone in an executive position, you'll have the opportunity to prove yourself to that person, and at the same time, gain additional experience.

Throughout your internship, go out of your way to help people and always be polite and respectful to everyone. Get to know your superiors and volunteer to stay late, if necessary, to get projects completed. Whatever you're assigned to do, make sure that your work is 100 percent accurate, and done in a timely manner. The faster you prove that you're responsible and motivated, the faster you'll be given more exciting responsibilities. Also, don't be afraid to ask questions. If you don't know how to complete a task, instead of making costly mistakes, ask for assistance from your supervisor or superior. It's always much easier to do something right the first time then it is to go back and fix mistakes.

After your internship comes to an end, get letters of recommendation from your supervisor(s) or superior(s). Also, stay in touch with these people. Once you begin your job search, they can be useful contacts for locating job opportunities. If you did you're best work during the internship, and proved that your a

capable and motivated person who worked well within the corporate structure of the company, you could ultimately wind up with a job offer from that company. Even if you don't get a job offer, you will have work experience in a specific industry that you can list on your resume.

As you begin thinking about internship opportunities, visit the career planning office at your college or university. There you can learn more about the types of internship programs that are available.

CHAPTER

28

DAY TRIPS
GETTING AWAY
FROM IT ALL

s a reward for all your hard work in school, once in a while you might want to grab your boyfriend/girl-friend, your best friend, or a group of friends and take a day trip, or do something that's non-school related and lots of fun.

If you can take a weekday off, or you're looking for an exciting activity for the weekend, here are some ideas for day trips that'll help you take your mind off the pressures of college. Obviously, some of these day trip ideas will cost money, and others are only applicable during certain times of the year, but no matter where you go, you'll be able to find some unusual and fun ways to spend a free day.

No matter what you wind up doing, remember to bring along your student I.D. card, because many of the day-trip destinations described in this chapter offer student discounts. Some of these destinations also offer less expensive admission prices during the week, while others offer coupons for discounted admission. Another way to save money on admission to one of the day-trip destinations described in this chapter is to gather a large group of friends together so you can obtain group discounts on admission and car pool to and from the destination.

Depending on your interests, there are many ways you can spend a day off from school that will require minimal planning. In addition to the ideas provided here, call the Department of Tourism in your city or state, check your local newspaper, and contact Ticket Master (or another ticket agency) for a listing of events happening in your area.

If you don't have a car available to get you to and from one of these destinations, consider:

- Renting a Car. Most rental car companies offer special one day rates or weekend rates. The minimum age for renting a car varies from state to state, so call a rental car agency in your area for details. When renting a car, spend the extra few bucks to purchase the insurance from the rental car agency. If you happen to get into an accident while driving a rental car, this insurance will protect you, yet your regular insurance rates won't go up.
- Take the Bus. All of the popular bus companies offer student discounts and provide hassle free and inexpensive transportation.
- Ride the Train/Subway/Commuter Rail. Whether you're traveling a short distance or between

states, the train is a great way to travel. Be sure to bring along homework, a Walkman, or a good book to help you pass the time.

○ Rent a Limo. If you get a group of friends together, most limo companies will offer a discount for long-distance travel. While taking a taxi is good for short distances, you want to work out a pre-determined, flat-rate with a limo company before you depart on a long-distance trip. Check your local phone book for the limo companies in your area.

○ Borrow a Car. As long as you have a driver's license, you can consider borrowing a car from a friend, however, should something happen to the car while it's in your possession, you will be responsible. Check with your insurance company to make sure you would be covered if you get into an accident while driving a borrowed car. (Borrowing a car means asking permission from the owner of the car. Without permission, you are technically stealing the car, even if you plan to return it when you're done.)

Amusement Parks and Water Parks

Just about everyone is just a few hours drive away from a major amusement park or theme park. To find smaller, locally owned and operated amusement parks, theme parks and water parks in your area on the Internet, check out FunGuide at http://www.funguide.com/parks/usa.html. These smaller parks probably don't offer the multi-million dollar rides and attractions or the fancy shows, but they're probably closer to your school and have lower admission fees.

Here are a few of the major amusement parks, theme parks, and water parks located throughout the country. Some of these attractions are seasonal (they're only open during certain months of the year) so call before making the trip.

○ The Walt Disney World Resort
(Orlando, Florida)—
(407) W-DISNEY
The Magic Kingdom
Epcot Center
The Disney/MGM Studios

Pleasure Island
The Disney Institute
Blizzard Beach
Typhoon Lagoon
○ Disneyland (Anaheim,
  California)—(714) 999-4565
  Disney's California Adventure—
  Opening in 2001
○ Knott's Berry Farm (Orange
  Country, California)—(714) 220-5200
○ Universal Studios Hollywood
  (Universal City, California)—(818)
  888-1000
○ Universal Studios Florida
  (Orlando, Florida)—(800) BE-A-
  STAR
○ Six Flags
  Six Flags Magic Mountain
    (Valencia, California)—
    (805) 255-4100
  Six Flags Great Adventure/Safari
    (Jackson, New Jersey)—(908)
    928-2000
  Six Flags Fiesta Texas (San
    Antonio, Texas)—(210) 697-5000
  Six Flags Over Georgia (Atlanta,
    Georgia)—(770) 948-9290
  Six Flags Great America (Gurnee,
    Illinois)—(847) 249-2133
  Six Flags Houston (Houston,
    Texas)—(713) 799-8404
  Six Flags Over Mid America
    (Eureka, Missouri)—(314) 938-5300
  Six Flags Over Texas (Arlington,
    Texas)—(817) 640-8900

Six Flags Wet and Wild
  (Arlington, Texas)—(817) 265-3356
○ Paramount Parks
  Paramount's Great America (Santa
    Clara, California)—(408) 988-1776
  Paramount's Kings Island
    (Cincinnati, Ohio)—(513) 398-5600
  Paramount's Carowinds
    (Charlotte, North Carolina)—
    (704) 588-2606
  Paramount's Kings Dominion
    (Richmond, Virginia)
    (804) 876-5000
  Paramount's Canada's
    Wonderland (Ontario, Canada)—
    (416) 832-7000
○ Busch Gardens and Sea World
  Adventure Island (Tampa,
    Florida)—(813) 987-5000
  Busch Gardens (Tampa Bay,
    Florida)—(813) 987-5171
  Busch Gardens (Williamsburg,
    Virginia)—(757) 253-3000
  Sea World (San Diego, CA)—
    (619) 222-6363
  Sea World (Orlando, Florida)—
    (407) 351-3600
  Sea World (Aurora, Ohio)—
    (216) 562-8101
  Sea World (San Antonio,
    Texas)—(512) 523-3611
  Water Country USA (Willamsburg,
    Virginia)—(757) 229-9300
○ Hersheypark (Hershey,
  Pennsylvania)—(800) HERSHEY

Theater and Concerts

Every year dozens of Broadway shows like *Rent*, *Grease*, *Joseph and the Technicolor Dreamcoat*, *Blue Man Group*, *Stomp*, *Phantom of the Opera*, and *Les Miserables* travel the country, most with casts made up of well-known, professional actors. Tickets to these shows often cost as much as seeing the show on Broadway in New York City, but matinee performances and student discounts offered by theaters will save you money. If you don't want to spend up to $70 per ticket to see a Broadway-quality show, you can check out the regional or non-professional theater groups and dinner theaters in your area.

The Ringling Brothers, Barnam & Bailey Circus, Stars On Ice, Ice Capades, David Copperfield, and many other shows constantly travel the country and offer an afternoon or evening's worth of quality entertainment at a reasonable cost. Be sure to ask about group discounts and student discounts before purchasing your tickets.

All of the big-name recording artists go on tour, and whether you're attending school in a major city, or in the middle of nowhere, there are always concerts you can attend. For a complete listing of upcoming concerts, contact TicketMaster (or another ticket agency), or call local theaters, concert halls, stadiums, and arenas directly. The local newspaper in your area most likely publishes complete concert and show listings on a weekly basis. Radio stations also promote upcoming concerts and offer concert tickets as prizes for contests. If you can't afford to buy concert tickets, keep listening and calling your favorite radio station and try to win some.

Museums, Aquariums and Other Tourist Attractions

Just about every city in America has museums, historical sites, an aquarium, botanical gardens, OMNI theaters, and other tourist attractions that can be fun to visit. To find out about these attractions, check a local telephone book, call the Department of Tourism in your area, or drop into a local hotel and check out the brochures that can almost always be found near the hotel's registration desk or concierge. Almost all museums, aquariums, and other tourist attractions offer student discounts.

Public Parks and Beaches

Spending the day at a park or at the beach is cheap, relaxing, and usually always enjoyable. Make sure you wear comfortable shoes and bring along plenty of sun tan lotion. You might also want to pack a picnic lunch and your in-line skates, a Frisbee, or a kite.

Road Trips To Another City

Sometimes is can be fun to get in your car and drive to another city or a distant destination, either for the day or for the weekend. If you or a friend has a reliable car, it's always fun to visit nearby cities and shop, visit tourist attractions, or just explore. If you're attending school in the Boston area, for example, some of the cities you might want to check out are: Providence, Rhode Island, Hartford, Connecticut, and New York City. (New York City is approximately a four-hour drive from Boston.) Road trips can also become part of another activity, such as a trip to an amusement park, or a weekend ski trip.

Ten Tips For Road-Trips

1. Make sure your car is capable of making the trip. If you know your car requires major repair work, get the work done before attempting a long drive.
2. Bring your AAA membership card (or auto club card) in case your car breaks down, and you need a tow or a flat tire replaced.
3. Before leaving, check the air in your tires, make sure you have gas, and make sure the spare tire is in working order. Depending on the weather, you should also top off your car's windshield washer fluid.
4. Pack snacks and drinks (or be prepared to make pit stops at fast food restaurants.) Obviously, don't pack any alcoholic beverages and never drink and drive.
5. Pack a few pillows and blankets. On long drives, you'll probably want to switch drivers multiple times. The person who isn't driving might want to get some sleep. Never drive when your

too tired. If necessary, pull into a rest stop and take a one- or two-hour nap.
6. Don't forget your radar detector (assuming it's legal to use one in the state or states you'll be driving in.)
7. Pack a change of clothes and bring along sun glasses. In case you get stuck, and wind up having to stay someplace overnight, or if you get stuck in snow or rain and get very wet, you'll want something clean and dry to change into.
8. Get accurate driving directions before you leave. Call AAA (or your auto club). Most auto clubs will provide detailed driving directions over the phone. Plan out your route on a map, or use navigation software on your computer.
9. Bring along some extra cash or a credit card in case you need more gas then you planned, in cas you need to get towed, or if some other emergency happens.
10. Make sure you keep a flashlight, jumper cables, emergency flares, and even a small first aid kit in your car. Also, bring along tapes and/or CDs so you have music to listen to.

Rollerblading® (In-Line Skating): Why Walk When You Can Skate?

In-line skating is definitely one of the fastest growing sports of the decade, and anyone can learn how to do it. You don't have to be athletic, strong, tall, or physically fit. Rollerblade®, Inc. is a leading manufacturer and marketer of in-line skates and related products. In case you're not familiar with in-line skates, they're a cross between ice skates and roller skates. While the skills required to master in-line skating and ice skating are very similar, in-line skates contain a single row of four wheels on the bottom of each skate, and the brakes for the skates are on the heel. Traditional roller skates have two wheels on each side of the skate; the wheels on in-line skates are in a row.

Just like any type of sporting equipment, there are many makes and models of in-line skates. Rollerblade® offers a wide selection of models, which range in price from about $100 to $400 a pair. Some models are designed for beginners, while others are more suitable for expert skaters or for roller hockey players (street hockey played on in-line skates.) Most sporting goods stores carry a selection of in-line skate models, so try on several pair and ask for assistance from someone who knows about them. Don't just settle for a pair of skates based on how they look or what they cost. Proper fit is critical, so don't think you can borrow a pair of skates from a friend who has a shoe size that is different from yours.

The coolest thing about in-line skating is that it feels like you're gliding through the air. Just like any sport, wearing the proper safety equipment is important. Rollerblade®, Inc. recommends wearing wrist guards, elbow pads, knee pads, and a helmet (a bicycle helmet works perfectly). For beginners, learning how to avoid falling down and mastering the art of turning and stopping is all part of the fun and challenge of this sport. Don't expect to put on a pair of in-line skates for the first time and skate like a pro. Even if you're an expert ice skater, learning to in-line skate is going to take practice.

An ideal way to get started is to take a lesson from a professional. In-line skating lessons are offered at many sporting goods stores. A typical person will only need one or two lessons to get started. Rollerblade® Inc. has teams of professional instructors that constantly tour the country and offer free lessons. Many adult education centers, community centers, and park programs also offer skating lessons. The company has also produced an instructional videocassette, called Ready, Set...Roll! that is sold at many Rollerblade® Inc. dealers. Books on how to in-line skate are available from most bookstores. As a beginner, your first job is to learn how to maintain your balance on the skates, initiate turns, and stop. Maintaining control and wearing the proper safety equipment will help you avoid injury.

If you love being outdoors especially, in-line skating is an excellent alternative to bike riding, walking, and hiking. For college students, in-line skating is perfect, because all of the equipment you need can be easily stored in your dorm room (unlike a bicycle), and the cost of the equipment is relatively in-expensive.

To learn more about Rollerblade® Inc. in-line skates and products, check out the Rollerblade® site on the Internet at http://www.rollerblade.com, or call (800) 232-ROLL.

Fun Places To In-Line Skate

Unlike bike riding, in-line skating is an awesome sport because you can do it almost anywhere where there is a paved surface. Never try skating on grass, on bumpy pavement, or in wet or icy conditions. If you skate to and from class, bring along a pair of shoes to change into when you get to class, and carry your skates with you once you reach your destination. Keep in mind, most stores, restaurants, and public buildings will not allow you to wear your skates inside, so wear a backpack and keep a pair of shoes handy. In addition to being an ideal form of transportation (for relatively short trips) in-line skating is also an awesome recreational sport. Some of the places you can skate include:

- Waterfront boardwalks or paved sidewalks
- Paved bike paths (often found in parks)

o Industrial parks (after hours or on weekends)

o Large, flat and empty parking lots that are paved

o Around your school's track (if it's permitted)

o Country roads and streets that aren't too busy. Until you've

become a good skater (someone who knows how to turn, stop, maintain balance, and stay in control at all times), avoid skating on public streets and avoid hills.

o Skating rinks (some roller skating rinks allow in-line skaters)

Bike Trips and Hiking

Whether you're attending school in a city, the suburbs, or in the country, chances are there are bike trails, hiking trails, and scenic places, such as parks, wildlife reserves, or along canals, to bike ride, walk, jog, hike or in-line skate. You can always rent a bike or a pair of in-line skates from a local bike shop. If you have a bike rack for your car (or a large trunk), you can drive to a new location and then spend the day biking, hiking, or in-line skating. These activities will provide you with a good escape from the daily grind of college, provide an opportunity to get fresh air and exercise, and provide inexpensive fun.

If you plan on biking, hiking, or skating for great distances, for long periods of time, or in isolated areas, make sure you tell someone where you're going and when you plan on

returning. (This is just good common sense in case something happens, someone will know where to search for you). Here are some of the essentials you'll want to bring along on long hikes or bike trips:

o Plenty of water

o A backpack or waist pack (to carry your stuff)

o Food or snacks

o Extra clothing

o A compass and a map

o A first-aid kit

o A flashlight

o Sun screen

o Rain gear

o A portable air pump for your bike (if applicable)

o A small tool kit for your bike (if applicable)

Before leaving on your hiking, walking, or bike trips, you might want to visit The Backpacker on the Internet at http://www.thebackpacker.com. This site offers articles, product reviews, and a large directory of destinations across America that are particularly scenic or ideal for day-long excursions.

Sports Events/A Day At The Races

If you're attending school in or near a city with professional sports teams, attending a day game can provide an excellent break from your school work. No matter what sport you like—football, basketball, hockey, or soccer—you can almost always purchase tickets for a home game at the stadium's box office the day of the game.

Spending the day (or evening) at a race track (dog races or horse races) is another exciting and relatively inexpensive way to spend some time. This type of activity gets more expensive, however, if you choose to place bets and you lose.

Down-Hill or Cross Country Skiing / Snowboarding

Any place where the climate gets cold in the winter months offers some type of skiing. Of course, you can travel to Colorado, Maine, Vermont, or one of the other major skiing locations in America, or you can check out the local ski slopes in your area. Many parks, wildlife reservations, and even some golf courses allow cross-country skiing as long as there's enough snow on the ground. If you don't own ski equipment, you can always rent it. If skiing is available in your area, the Department of Tourism probably offers a ski conditions phone number. You can also call ski slopes directly for the latest conditions.

Down-hill skiing and snowboarding are expensive sports, even if you own your own equipment. A one-day lift ticket can cost between $20 and $40 depending on the ski slope. However, almost all slopes offer student discounts and lower lift ticket rates on weekdays. If you've never been skiing before, it's never too late to learn, but it's an excellent idea to sign up for a lesson from a professional instructor. Even if your friends offer to give you free ski lessons, start off by taking a private or group lesson from a professional instructor at a ski slope—then let your friends give you lessons.

If you're lucky enough to go skiing often, but you don't want to invest several hundred dollars in a new pair of skis, bindings, and ski boots, you should consider purchasing secondhand equipment. Many ski equipment dealers also offer huge discounts if you buy your equipment off-season (during non-winter months) or if you buy last year's models.

To find places to ski, learn the latest ski conditions, read about the latest skiing and snowboarding equipment, or get tips for skiing, check out these Web sites on the Internet:

- Snow-Bound—http://www.snow-bound.com
- HyperSki—http://www.hyperski.com
- Yahoo! Ski Report—http://la.yahoo.com/external/ami
- Ami On-The-Go—http://www.aminews.com/ski
- Ski Magazine & Skiing Magazine On-line—http://www.skinet.com

Horseback Riding

Even if you're not a cowboy or cowgirl, spending a day horseback riding can be a blast! There are stables located everywhere, so check your local phone book. You and your friends might want to take a riding lesson, or just visit a stable and go on a group horseback riding tour. Just about anyone can learn the basics of horseback riding in a very short amount of time, and the cost for this activity is relatively low. Make sure you wear long pants (or jeans) when horseback riding.

Visit a Local Casino

Local casinos are popping up in cities and on Indian reservations across America. In fact, over thirty-one states now have legal casinos. To find the casinos in your state, check out Casio City on the Internet (http://www. casinocity.com). No longer is it necessary to visit Las Vegas or Atlantic City if you want to try your luck playing poker, blackjack, craps, roulette, the slot machines, or another casino game. In addition to gambling, many of these casinos offer restaurants, shows, and other attractions that make for a fun day and/or night.

How much this activity costs depends on how much you're willing to gamble. Before you step into a casino, determine how much money you are willing to lose—$10, $20, $50 or more, and be prepared to leave the casino and head back to school once you lose that amount of money. If you get on a winning streak, set a time limit for how long you want to stay. If you win early in the day and then keep gambling, unless you're incredibly lucky, chances are you're eventually going to lose the money you've won.

A Day of Beauty

Spending time at a spa or salon will probably appeal mainly to females and cost a good amount of money. But if you need to relax and reward yourself by being pampered, have a facial, massage, manicure and/or sitting in a whirl pool. It's well-worth the investment. The prices for these services vary greatly depending on the salon or spa you visit, so call in advance and find out what services are offered and how much they cost. To find a spa or salon in your area, check a local telephone book. A growing number of expensive hotels are also adding spas that are available to gusts and non-guests alike.

TicketMaster Can Be Your Entertainment Guide

Just about any type of show, sporting event, or activity that takes place in a theater, stadium, or arena offers tickets through a national ticket agency, such as TicketMaster. By contacting a ticket agency, you can obtain an up-to-date listing of activities happening in your area. You can almost always save money by buying your tickets directly from the box office of the theater, stadium, or arena. Ticket agencies, such as TicketMaster, often charge rather hefty service fees if you buy your tickets through them. The benefit to these services is that you can purchase tickets in advance, over the telephone, and avoid waiting in long lines.

TicketMaster On-line is a free service available on the Internet (www.ticket master.com) that offers complete listings for events happening in all major cities and states. By visiting http://events.ticket-master.com, you can access a listing of events happening in your specific area. TicketMaster On-line is available whether or not you purchase your tickets through this service.

Need More Day Trip Ideas? Check with AAA!

Membership to the American Automobile Association (AAA) is probably one of the all-time best deals available for someone who owns or operates a car. If you're planning a day trip, your AAA membership can help you determine where you want to go, get you to your destination, and provide you with discounts on admission. Should your car happen to break down along the way, AAA will also come to the rescue.

Aside from helping stranded motorists jump-start their battery, change a flat tire, or provide a tow to a nearby garage, AAA can provide all sorts of travel information. To take advantage of any AAA travel service, membership is required, so call (800) 222-4357 for information, or check out AAA On-line (http://www.aaa.com) or on America On-line (keyword: AAA).

If you're planning a road trip, have an AAA Travel Office provide you with a customized Triptik® Routing. You provide your starting location and your destination, and AAA provides you with detailed driving directions on how to get there by car. In addition, your Triptik will include up-to-date information to help you make the most of your road trip, by providing exit numbers, rest areas, food stops, gas stations, detailed maps, and summaries of towns and cities on the route. Triptiks are provided free of charge to members.

AAA also publishes a series of twenty-three TourBooks®, and eight Destination Guides which are offered free of charge upon request. TourBooks® are filled with listings of attractions, lodgings, and restaurants throughout America. These books will provide dozens of day trip ideas, details about attractions, and offer pricing and discount information for each attraction. Currently, TourBooks® are available for the following regions and states:

○ Alabama/Louisiana/Mississippi
○ Arizona/New Mexico
○ Arkansas/Kansas/Missouri/ Oklahoma
○ Atlantic Provinces and Quebec
○ California/Nevada
○ Colorado/Utah
○ Connecticut/Massachusetts/ Rhode Island
○ Florida

- Georgia/North Carolina/South Carolina
- Hawaii
- Idaho/Montana/Wyoming
- Illinois/Indiana/Ohio
- Kentucky/Tennessee
- Maine/New Hampshire/Vermont
- Michigan/Wisconsin
- Mid-Atlantic (Delaware, District of Columbia, Maryland, Virginia and West Virginia)
- New Jersey/Pennsylvania
- New York
- North Central (Iowa, Minnesota, Nebraska, North Dakota and South Dakota)
- Ontario
- Oregon/Washington State
- Texas
- Western Canada and Alaska

AAA Destination Guides offer in-depth coverage of several major U.S. cities. If you happen to be attending school in Chicago, Los Angeles, Miami, New Orleans, New York, San Francisco, Tampa, or Washington, D.C., the *AAA Destination Guide* for that city will provide you with everything you need to know about the city, including maps, and countless ideas for day trips within that city. Similar books, published by Frommer's, EconoGuides and other book publishers are available at bookstores everywhere, but you'll have to pay for them.

Your AAA membership can save you money at popular hotels (Clarion Hotels & Resorts, Comfort Inns, Days Inn, Econo Lodge, Hilton, Hyatt, La Quinta Inns, Rodeway Inns, and Sleep Inns), when renting a car (at Hertz or Ryder) or at dozens of amusement parks and attractions.

At any Six Flags Theme Park, show your membership card and receive $4 off the price of an adult admission ticket. You can also receive a Triple Discount on Wednesdays. Check with any AAA Travel Office (located throughout America) for additional savings coupons.

When visiting any Sea World or Busch Gardens theme park, AAA members will save 10 percent of the admission price, plus an additional 10 percent off selected souvenirs and dining.

Universal Studios Hollywood and Florida offer a $3 discount off the price of admission to AAA members, and a 10 percent savings on selected souvenirs and dining.

If you are planning to travel by train, use your AAA membership card to obtain a 10 percent discount off the lowest available fare on any Amtrak train.

CHAPTER

29

THE ULTIMATE SPRING BREAK VACATION

LET THE BUYER BEWARE

The biggest piece of advice college students need when booking their Spring Break travel plans is to beware of deals that are too good to be true. On the bulletin boards all around your college campus and in your school's newspaper, you'll see colorful ads for special Spring Break travel packages offered by tour operators. The majority of these travel packages are totally legit. However, if a company is offering you a week in Daytona Beach, Florida, or Cancun, Mexico, with round-trip airfare and hotel at an outrageously low rate . . . beware!

Inexperienced travelers should consult a licensed travel agent when planning a Spring Break vacation. Travel agents know all of the "hot spots" and what special deals are available. All of the major airlines also offer package deals to various vacation destinations. Finally, there are travel companies that cater specifically to college students and do nothing but offer special Spring Break packages. Again, the majority of these companies are legit, but some of them aren't. So before paying your money (which is often nonrefundable) and booking your travel arrangements (which is often nonchangeable) speak to people you know who have had good experiences working with the travel company/tour operator you have in mind.

Whether or not you book your travel arrangements directly with the airline and the hotel, work with a travel agent, or take advantage of the offers from a Spring Break tour operator, do as much research as possible before you leave. Go to the library or a bookstore and pick up a travel guide for the city or country where you'll be vacationing. A travel guide will list all of the major tourist attractions, hotels, nightclubs, and even bars and ultimately help you to make the most out of your vacation. Even if you're planning to simply hang out at the beach during the day and go clubbing at night, wouldn't you like to insure that you're sunning at the nicest beaches and partying the most popular night spots?

The advantage of booking a travel package is that the tour operators get excellent deals, because they buy rooms and airfares in bulk. Often they pass along the savings to you. In addition, tour operators often offer special discounts at local clubs, restaurants, and tourist attractions. When booking a package, ask up front (and get it in writing), what is covered and what isn't. Just because a hotel/resort offers activities such as scuba diving, surfing, parasailing, sailing, and jet-skis doesn't mean that the cost of these activities is included in your package. You could wind up paying very high prices for them. Likewise, you should ask what meals, if any, are included, and if these meals are provided by your hotel restaurant or by another restaurant. Also ask about your hotel. What amenities/services are offered? Where is the hotel located in relation to the beaches, bars, clubs, and so forth? Does the tour operator have an on-site representative at your vacation destination that can assist you with problems, should any arise? Read all of the fine print. Also, ask about additional taxes and extra costs before booking your travel.

The biggest disadvantage to booking a Spring Break vacation through a tour operator is that your travel plans cannot be changed and there are no refunds. Thus, if you arrive at your destination and the weather is awful, you're stuck there. If you book your own travel, you can always cancel your hotel or change your airline reservations at the last minute; some restrictions will apply, and you could be charged a fee for making

changes, but at least you're not stuck. Booking your own travel may turn out to be a bit more costly (since you can't take advantage of package deals and specials), but if you need to be flexible, it might be worth it.

When booking your hotel, be prepared to pay a damage deposit (in cash) in advance. Obviously, if you leave the hotel room the way you found it, your money will be refunded.

Sure, consuming alcohol and partying during your Spring Break vacation is considered normal, but it is not required. At most destinations in Mexico, the drinking age is eighteen, but it's not heavily enforced, especially during Spring Break. To protect yourself, never leave your friends and party with a group of strangers. Also, if you're female, don't get so drunk that you could find yourself in a potentially dangerous situation. Statistics show that about one out of four college-age women get raped or sexually assaulted during their college years. Protect yourself! But, should anything happen, report it immediately, or at the very least, get medical attention and confidential counseling for yourself—no matter where you are or what time it is.

No matter what, NEVER purchase, use, obtain, or carry illegal drugs, especially if you're vacationing in another country. This is illegal, and drug laws are enforced just about everywhere. You don't want to find yourself arrested and in jail in a foreign country. If this does happen, contact your parents and the American embassy in that country immediately. Don't try to deal with the situation yourself.

Always carry a picture identification and a small amount of cash with you wherever you go. Also, once you arrive at your destination, keep a piece of paper in your wallet that lists your hotel phone number and address, along with the phone number of a local taxi company, in case you get stranded somewhere.

Following is a list of some of the hottest Spring Break destinations:

○ Daytona Beach, Florida
○ Panama City Beach, Florida
○ Cancun, Mexico
○ South Padre Island, Texas
○ Myrtle Beach, Florida
○ Key West, Florida
○ Clearwater/St. Petersberg, Florida
○ Ft. Lauderdale, Florida
○ South Miami Beach, Florida
○ A Cruise (Carnival Cruise Lines)
○ Mazatlan, Mexico
○ The Bahamas
○ Jamaica
○ Wherever MTV happens to be broadcasting from during Spring Break

Here are some suggestions on ways to save money when planning your vacation:

○ Book a hotel that has a kitchen or kitchenette so you can cook some of your own meals.
○ Reserve a hotel room with two or three friends and split the cost. Don't rent a room for just two or four people, for example, and then invite large groups of people to stay there. There are laws that protect the hotel operators, and you could get thrown out of the hotel, but still have to pay for your entire stay. Most hotels will allow a maximum of four people to stay in a room. You can get the best package deals if you're traveling as a group of four people (you and three friends).
○ Beware of phone charges from your hotel room! You could be billed outrageous charges for making calls. Your best bet is to always use a pay phone and use a calling card or prepaid calling card that you know offers an excellent rate. Making international collect calls home costs you nothing, but the people you're calling could receive a huge bill. To use AT&T, dial

1-(800) CALL-ATT (within the U.S.) from any phone. Avoid extra charges from "lesser known" phone companies.

○ Book a hotel that's not right on but is within walking distance to the beach. You'll pay a premium for being right on a beach.

○ Ask about student discounts at stores, night clubs, restaurants, bars, and so on. Don't forget to bring along your college ID.

○ When eating out, look for all-you-can-eat buffets and places that offer lunch or dinner specials.

Here are some suggestions on things to do before you leave:

○ Start planning your Spring Break vacation one or two months prior to departure. Don't wait until the last minute!

○ Go to the bank and get travelers checks and use them instead of cash. Don't carry large amounts of cash with you when traveling. No matter what, plan on spending more money then the prices quoted for the trip. Bring along a credit card, even if it's only for emergencies. You may want to shop, do extra activities,

upgrade your hotel, rent a car, and so forth.

○ All expensive jewelry and valuables should be left at home.

○ Call the airline and hotel directly to confirm your reservation and your rates. Don't rely on a tour operator or travel agent to do this for you. Make sure you have your hotel confirmation number or confirmation slip with you.

○ Make sure your passport is current (if you're traveling to Mexico or outside of the U.S.).

No matter where you wind up going on vacation, plan your trip in advance. While you're there, have fun, but be smart!

Inter-Campus Programs, Inc., is a Chicago-based Spring Break tour operator that offers college student package deals to many of the top Spring Break destinations. Each year, Inter-Campus Programs helps over 15,000 students plan their vacations. Over the past decade, the company has worked with over 150,000 college students. For more information, call (800) 828-7015.

Don't Forget about Disney World for Spring Break Getaways

When most people think of Spring Break, what comes to mind are late-night parties, getting drunk, and those awful hangovers the next morning. That's how some people choose to spend their Spring Break vacation; but when they get home, their memories are virtually nonexistent. For those who don't drink, or don't live for parties, there are many Spring Break vacation alternatives that can provide an exciting and fun atmosphere, alternatives that don't evolve totally around alcohol.

The Walt Disney World Resort (WDW) in Orlando, Florida, isn't just for young kids or families anymore. Everyone who has vacationed there as a child has fond memories of the Magic Kingdom, Epcot Center, the Disney-MGM Studios, and the Disney water parks, but there's so much more to do at WDW when you're older.

With the expansion of Pleasure Island and the opening of Disney's Boardwalk, you can experience all of Disney's most popular theme parks, water parks, and attractions by day, and then party at night at one of the many clubs, bars, and night time hot spots that are for adults (eighteen and older) only.

Each year, Disney offers several different discount packages specifically for college students, which include hotel, airfare, theme park admission, food, and access to Pleasure Island. To find out what types of discount packages are available, call (407) W-DISNEY. To get the most out of your Disney vacation, stay at one of Disney's twenty-seven hotels and resorts. This way, you're in the heart of the action, both day and night, and you don't have to rent a car. The All-Star Sports Resort and All-Star Music Resort offer the cheapest on-property room rates, but you'll have to book your reservations early. Just off of Disney's 30,000+ acre site, you'll find dozens of independent and chain hotels, motels, and resorts, many of which offers free shuttle service to WDW.

If you stay at a Disney-owned hotel, you'll have access to dozens of different

---

sports and activities outside of the theme parks, which you can participate in during the day. Boating, hiking, rock climbing, scuba diving, swimming, fishing, water skiing, tennis, golf, parasailing, and just about any other outdoor activity you can image is offered somewhere on Disney property. Of course, the Disney theme parks also offer many thrill rides—such as Tower of Terror, Test Track, The ExtraTERRORestrial Alien Encounter, Space Mountain, Splash Mountain, and, of course, It's a Small World. The new 500-acre Animal Kingdom (opening in Spring 1998) allows you to get close to over 1,000 live animals. And when you want to splash around on a hot day, there are three different Disney water parks to visit.

When night falls, head for Pleasure Island! The Disney Imagineers, who create the attractions at the Disney theme parks, discovered a few years ago that there wasn't a whole lot to do at night, especially for adults visiting the Walt Disney World Resort. As a result, in 1989, Pleasure Island opened, and its been expanding ever since. Every night at midnight, you can catch a special live show and fireworks display at Pleasure Island. This is a totally separate area of the Walt Disney World Resort. It contains several nightclubs, bars, and restaurants including:

- ○ Mannequins. Mannequins features a large rotating floor, a state-of-the-art sound and light system, and a full bar.
- ○ Rock 'N Roll Beach Club. You'll want to check out this huge, three-floor dance club that plays rock 'n roll music from the 50s to the present.
- ○ 8-Trax. 8-Trax is a dance club and bar that features music from the 70s and 80s.
- ○ The Comedy Warehouse. At the Comedy Warehouse, an improv troupe performs several shows nightly and invites audience participation.
- ○ The Neon Armadillo. Here you'll find live country music, a DJ and

nonstop dancing with a country twist.

○ Adventurers Club. This club offers a bar and a rather unusual comedy show.

○ Pleasure Island Jazz Club. Some of the biggest jazz musicians in the world travel to Pleasure Island to perform at this intimate club.

○ Planet Hollywood Orlando. See props and costumes from Hollywood's biggest movies as you dine and drink at this trendy hot spot.

○ Lario's Night Club. Owned by Gloria Estefan, here's another exciting party location.

○ House of Blues. Live musical performances, food, and drink are offered here.

○ AMC Movie Theaters. You can see all of the latest movies at this twenty-four-screen movie theater complex located at Pleasure Island.

One flat cover charge (if it's not included in your vacation package) gives you access to all of the clubs at Pleasure Island. Of course, beverages and food are extra.

The late-night parties and excitement continue at Disney's Boardwalk, where you can find additional dance clubs, the

THERE'S PLENTY MORE TO DO WHILE VACATIONING IN ORLANDO

Also in the Orlando area are Universal Studios Florida, Sea World, and many other attractions that'll keep you entertained during the daylight hours, as you get ready for the Spring Break nightlife. Universal Studios Florida, like WDW, is constantly expanding and adding new attractions, like TERMINATOR 2 3-D. Universal City Travel Company has been formed to offer vacationers all-inclusive packages that include accommodations, unlimited free transportation between hotels and parks, airfare, car rental, and unlimited visits to Universal Studios Florida, Sea World of Florida, and Wet 'N Wild. For an additional fee, tickets to WDW can also be added to the packages offered by Universal City Travel. To find out more about these travel packages to Orlando, contact a travel agent, or call (407) 224-7000. You can also check out Universal Studio Florida's Internet site at http://www.usf.com.

ESPN Sports Club, Jellyroll's Dueling Piano Bar, Big River Grille & Brewing Works, and lots more.

Sports, theme parks, water parks, dancing, drinking, shows, and dining—The Walt Disney World Resort in Orlando, Florida, truly offers something for everyone. You can spend a portion of your vacation perfecting your tennis game, or you can learn something new, like how to rock climb, use self-defense, surf the Internet, draw an animated character, or cook a romantic dinner. You can sign up for classes at the Disney Institute. Dozens of interesting and exciting classes are offered at this totally unique Disney resort.

To learn more about the latest Disney vacations, attractions, and night spots, check out Disney On-Line at http://www.disney.com. You can also contact the Florida Tourism Office and obtain a free Florida vacation kit by calling (904) 487-1462.

Enjoy Your Vacation, But Spend Less!

One of the best travel tips anyone can offer is to shop around for the best deals, and keep your eyes open for coupons that run in the travel sections of newspapers. If you live or plan to travel to one of 165 U.S. cities, or Amsterdam, London, Paris, Stockholm, Mexico City, or Australia, then you might want to get your hands on an Entertainment Book Discount Travel Guide. Published by Entertainment Publications, Inc., Entertainment books are published yearly, and include thousands of coupons and special offers from hotels, rental car companies, airlines, restaurants, shops, health clubs, night clubs, sporting attractions, amusement parks, and movie theaters.

For between $23 and $48, you can purchase an Entertainment book for a specific city, and it's good for one year. If you're planning a trip, use the Entertainment Book and save up to 50 percent on every meal, plus save serious money on virtually every other aspect of your trip. In the past thirty-seven years, over 5.5 million Entertainment books have been sold, and over 100,000 merchants have offered discount coupons or special offers.

Also available from Entertainment Publications is the Ultimate Travel and

Savings Directory, which offers discounts of up to 50 percent at more than 5,500 hotels worldwide. This 328-page directory also offers discounts on tourist attractions, such as Busch Gardens, Sea World, Cypress Gardens, Adventure Island USA, Water Country USA, and Six Flags Theme Parks, plus discounts on airfares, cruises, and rental cars.

To obtain many of the discounts offered in the various Entertainment books, you must book your reservations early, since most hotels, for example, only allocate a small number of rooms with the 50 percent discount. When booking hotels out of state, contact the hotels directly for the best rates (instead of calling a hotel chain's toll-free reservation number). All hotel phone numbers are listed.

To find out more about the various Entertainment books, call (800) 445-4137. You might also want to pick up the edition of the book for the city in which you're attending school, since you can save money at restaurants, movies, and even on your dry cleaning. In addition to Entertainment Publications, other companies offer similar travel discounts. The American Automobile Association (AAA), American Express, and Diner's Club all offer travel services and special offers that you can take advantage of when planning any type of travel or vacation.

CHAPTER

30

SUMMER SCHOOL & TRANSFERRING

ALTERNATIVES TO THE REGULARLY SCHEDULED PROGRAM

An alternative to taking classes during the normal school year is to take them during the summer. Unfortunately, you'll have to pass up spending hot summer days at the beach, but attending school during the summer is an ideal way to make up classes or to get ahead.

Many students begin their four-year college education at one school, and then transfer to another school and graduate. Others kick off their college education at a two-year school and later transfer to a four-year college or university. Whatever your reason is for transferring between schools, there are certain things you should know. One of the biggest drawbacks to transferring is that you'll lose credits on your transcript; and taking summer classes to make up for those losses may become necessary if you want to graduate on time.

This chapter explores the benefits and drawbacks of summer classes. It also offers some useful advice to students thinking about transferring schools.

Summer School

When you think of summer school, you may think of it as your worst nightmare coming true. After all, who wants to spend those gorgeous summer days sitting in a stuffy classroom being lectured at, or worse, in the library studying. Why would anyone in their right mind want to take classes over the summer? Well, here are a few good reasons:

- To make up an incomplete you received for a class or to retake a class you failed
- To get ahead (and graduate early)
- To become extra smart (and because you have no life)
- To take a reduced course load during the main school year, but still graduate on time

Despite what you might think, summer school doesn't last all summer. In addition, when you get right down to it, many of the professors teaching the summer classes dread being there just about as much as you do! As a result, at many college and university summer classes, the atmosphere is a bit more laid back and casual. In fact, summer school can actually be fun—the classes are smaller and less formal, and because of the time limitations, the information is often compressed. In addition, you have less time to forget what you've learned. So, before the final exam, you don't have to spend time relearning stuff from the beginning of the course. Most schools won't admit this, but summer classes are often easier and less stressful; so if there's a difficult course that you're dreading, consider taking in during a summer session.

Whether summer school is being forced on you or you just want to get ahead, one way to make it a bit more exciting is to take classes at another college or university. For example, if you currently attend a school in the New England area, find a class at a school like UCLA in Los Angeles, and take your summer class(es) there. When you're not in class, you can hang out at the beach. If you plan your summer courses well, you can schedule classes on Mondays, Wednesdays, and Fridays, or just Tuesdays and

Thursdays, so you'll have plenty of free time.

If you want to take summer classes at another school or educational institution, keep in mind that you'll have to coordinate everything with the transfer office at your school—before the summer session begins. Make sure that the class(es) you wish to take are transferable. Chances are, you'll need a course catalog and/or the course syllabus. Get the catalog and/or syllabus before you register for classes. Start planning early to ensure that you can reserve a dorm room and have plenty of time to make the necessary travel arrangements.

During the summer, some schools offer ultra-condensed one-week courses in which for that week, you live and breath one subject. The classes are all day, and often run into the evening, but only last for a week; and once it's over, you receive full credit for the course (assuming you pass.) The great thing about these one-week courses is that you have no time to forget what you've been taught, because the "semester" begins on Monday, you have a mid-term exam on Wednesday, and your final exam is on Friday. Yes, by the time the week is over, you'll feel totally brain dead; but if you want to complete an entire course quickly, and your school offers these one-week courses, consider this alternative.

Obviously, summer school is a lot more tolerable if you can gather up a few of your friends to join you, so you have people to hang out with after classes. You'll probably find that even at the biggest schools, the campus is pretty dead during the summer; the only people around are those taking summer classes. For evening and weekend entertainment, you'll probably have to go off campus.

Transferring to Another School: The Possibilities are Endless

If you happen to make the wrong decision about which college or university to attend, the good news is that you can always transfer to another school. Reasons to transfer might include:

○ Thanks to your earning excellent grades, you can now get into an Ivy League School (or a more competitive school).
○ You're changing your major, and want a school that better serves your interests.
○ You simply don't like the school you're attending.

○ You have financial considerations. (Perhaps you qualify for a scholarship at another school.)
○ You're not cutting it from an academic standpoint at your current school, and you want to transfer before flunking out. (If this is the case, before transferring, consider meeting with an academic advisor at your current school, taking a reduced course load, and/or getting tutored.)

Every school has a transfer office, which not only acts as an admissions office for transfer students but also helps transfer students get acquainted and succeed in their new school. One of the first steps you should take if you're considering a transfer is to think about the timing. Most schools only accept new transfer students at the start of a new semester, but you have to start your application process early. Next, contact the transfer office at the school(s) you're interested in applying to, and request an application and related information.

One thing you should seriously consider is which courses and how much course credit can be transferred to your new school. Every school has different rules and criteria for allowing credits to be transferred, and most schools will require that you retake certain courses, even if you earned passing grades in them at your original school. Most schools won't allow you to transfer a class in which you earned less than a C (or a B for more competitive schools) for a final grade.

Likewise, all schools have a limit as to how much credit you can transfer.

Thus, it is critical that before you actually transfer to a new school, you determine how much class credit (and which classes) can be transferred to your new school, or else you could wind up retaking a lot of classes, and delaying your graduation by one or more semesters. Take the time as you evaluate schools to request information about the degree requirements you'll need to achieve in order to graduate.

After you transfer to another school, it will take time to get acclimated to your new environment. Once again, you will be leaving your old friends behind and going into a new environment filled with strangers. The social scene, the classes, and the dorm life at your new school will be, without a doubt, different from your old school, so be prepared for different experiences.

Millions of students transfer to new schools each semester, but if you're going to be one of those students, make sure that the transfer will benefit you in the long run. Are you changing schools for the right reasons? Can you afford to lose credits and retake classes, even if it means graduating a semester or two later? Are you confident that you're going to enjoy and succeed at the new school you're transferring to? These are questions you should consider as you explore your transfer options.

Study Abroad

Almost every college or university offers its students the opportunity to study abroad for a semester and earn credits at the same time. In some cases, your school might offer a specific exchange program with another college or university overseas. If your school doesn't offer an organized study abroad program, contact your school's student affairs or transfer office and ask about opportunities that are available through other organizations. You might have to approach the overseas school directly, request a course catalog, and get whatever classes you hope to take overseas preapproved by your college or university in order to receive credit for them. Keep in mind that most colleges and universities won't allow you to transfer credits after your junior year, so if you're hoping to study abroad, for a semester or for a full year, consider doing it during your sophomore or junior year.

Taking college-level courses in another country can be an incredible experience. You'll have the opportunity to explore a new and different country and way of life. In fact, what you learn outside of the classroom during your time studying abroad could prove to be more educational than the classes you take.

To find out about the various study abroad programs available to American students, visit the Internet's World Wide Web, and using any search engine, enter the keywords study abroad. Or contact the transfer office at your school.

Index